20

PHILIP ALL
LITERATURE
FOR GCSE

PURPLE HIBISCUS
CHIMAMANDA NGOZI ADICHIE

Susan Elkin

Series editor: Jeanette Weatherall

 **PHILIP ALLAN**
UPDATES

L

Philip Allan Updates, an imprint of Hodder Education, an Hachette UK company, Market Place, Deddington, Oxfordshire OX15 0SE

Orders

Bookpoint Ltd, 130 Milton Park, Abingdon, Oxfordshire OX14 4SB
tel: 01235 827827
fax: 01235 400401
e-mail: education@bookpoint.co.uk
Lines are open 9.00 a.m.–5.00 p.m., Monday to Saturday, with a 24-hour message answering service. You can also order through the Philip Allan Updates website: www.philipallan.co.uk

P01789

Contents

Getting the most from this book and website

You may find it useful to read sections of this guide when you need them, rather than reading it from start to finish. For example, you may find it useful to read the *Context* section before you start reading the novel, or to read the *Plot and structure* section in conjunction with the novel — whether to back up your first reading of it at school or college or to help you revise. The *Tackling the assessments* section will be especially useful in the weeks leading up to the exam.

The following features have been used throughout this guide:

Target your thinking

● **What are the novel's main themes?**

A list of **introductory questions** to target your thinking is provided at the beginning of each chapter. Look back at these once you have read the chapter and check you have understood each of them before you move on.

Build critical skills

Broaden your thinking about the text by answering the questions in the **Pause for thought** boxes. They are intended to encourage you to consider your own opinions in order to develop your skills of criticism and analysis.

Pause for thought

Grade-boosting advice

Pay particular attention to the **Grade booster** boxes. Students with a firm grasp of these ideas are likely to be aiming for the top grades.

Grade *booster*

Key quotations are highlighted for you, and you may wish to use these as evidence in your examination answers. Page references are given for the 2009 paperback edition of *Purple Hibiscus* published by Fourth Estate (ISBN 978-0-00-718988-5).

> **Key quotation**
>
> **...it was not just the figurines that came tumbling down, it was everything.**
> (Kambili, p. 15)

Be exam-ready

The **Grade focus** sections explain how you may be assessed and distinguish between higher and foundation responses.

Grade *focus*

Get the top grades

Use the **Text focus** boxes to practise evaluating the text in detail and looking for evidence to support your understanding.

Text **focus**

Develop evaluation skills

Review your learning

Test your knowledge

Use the **Review your learning** sections to test your knowledge after you have read each chapter. Answers to the questions are provided in the final section of the guide.

 Don't forget to go online for even more free revision activities and self-tests:
www.philipallan.co.uk/literatureguidesonline

Introduction

Approaching the text

A novel is, above all, a narrative. A large part of the storyteller's art is to make you want to find out what happens next, and therefore to keep you reading to the end. In order to study *Purple Hibiscus,* and to enjoy it, you need to keep a close track of the events that take place. This guide will help you to do that, but you may also benefit from keeping your own notes on the main events and who is involved in them.

However, any novel consists of much more than its events. You need to know the story well to get a good grade in the exam, but if you spend a lot of time simply retelling the story you will not get a high mark. You also need to keep track of a number of other features:

- You need to consider the setting of the novel — where the events take place — and how this influences the story.
- You need to get to know the characters and how the author, Chimamanda Ngozi Adichie (pronounced 'a-dee-key'), reveals to us what they are like. Consider what they say and do and what other people say about them. Also think about why they behave in the way they do — their motives — and what clues the author gives us about this.
- As you read on, you will also notice themes — the ideas explored by the author. You may find it easier to think about these while not actually reading the book, especially if you discuss them with other people.
- You should also try to become aware of the style of the novel, especially on a second reading. This refers to how the writer presents the story.

All these aspects of the novel are dealt with in this guide. However, you should always try to notice them for yourself. This guide is no substitute for a careful and thoughtful reading of the text.

Revising the text

You will by now have read *Purple Hibiscus* at least once, almost certainly as part of class work or homework, backed up by various lessons and tasks at school to help you understand and get to know the text. Your job now is to revise it for your GCSE examination.

Key quotation

Things started to fall apart at home when my brother, Jaja, did not go to communion and Papa flung his heavy missal across the room and broke the figurines on the étagère.

(Kambili, p. 3)

The first thing to do is to reread the story to remind yourself what happens, who the characters are and how the novel is written. Ideally, before you take an English Literature exam, you need to have read the text right through at least three times.

If you find it difficult to make yourself sit down to read, one possibility is to read one section, or part of a section, a day alongside revision for other subjects. Although *Purple Hibiscus* is not divided into numbered chapters, there are 17 clearly separated sections and the book is presented in four parts. At a rate of one section every two days — or half a section each day — that is just over a month's fairly light work. If you begin early, you could do that before you start any more detailed revision.

Once you have reread the novel, you can begin to revise in more depth. This means looking at the story more closely, section by section. Many students find that they know the beginning of a novel better than the end, perhaps because they have begun to reread it several times but have failed to finish it. One way around this when revising chapters is to start from the end and work backwards. You already know the story, so you should be able to pick it up anywhere and know what is going on. This technique will not work for everyone, but many GCSE students find it helpful. Another possibility is to start in the middle, say at p. 141, and reread the second half before going back to the beginning.

> ## Grade *booster*
>
> The study of English Literature is an unending journey. The more you look, and the more work you do, the more you find, the more satisfying it is and the higher your eventual grade is likely to be. That is why this guide asks questions and expects you to work out your own answers.

Making the most of this guide

Read the *Context* section, which gives information on the historical, cultural and literary background of *Purple Hibiscus*. Most of what you write in your exam essay will relate directly to your reading of the text, but you will also get credit for showing that you understand something about the circumstances that gave rise to this novel. It is useful to know, for example, that Adichie was herself born in Nigeria in 1977 and that she still lives there. Your insights into *Purple Hibiscus* will be much more perceptive if you make an effort to understand the place and period.

When you are revising the novel section by section, use the *Plot and structure* section of this guide. Every novel has a shape. *Purple Hibiscus* is a well-crafted example. The plot summaries will help you to make sure that you have grasped the key elements of each chapter.

Once you have reminded yourself of the plot, you need to think about the novel as a whole and to build on the work that you have done in class about characters, themes and style. It is helpful to think of the 'big picture'. Studying short sections is the 'small picture', whereas looking at, say, how

Adichie develops the theme of family or the character of Papa, or how she maintains interest in her story, are examples of the 'big picture'.

Look carefully at the information provided in the *Characterisation*, *Themes* and *Style* sections of this guide, but remember that this is only a starting point. This guide does not contain everything you might need to write in an exam answer on *Purple Hibiscus*. Instead, it shows you what to look for, with plenty of examples. You should then, for instance, be able to find other themes in the novel or other interesting aspects of Adichie's language.

This guide ends with advice on how to tackle the GCSE exam by providing sample essays. It is best to work through the main body of the guide before you look at these. Once you really know the novel well, answering the exam questions should not present too much difficulty for most students. However, there are ways in which you can improve your essay-writing technique. Therefore, in the *Tackling the assessments* section, you will find advice on how to begin and end essays and how to make the best use of quotations. In the *Sample essays* section, you will find examples of A* answers to typical AQA questions, followed by grade C essays to show you the difference.

At the end of each section, 'Review your learning' questions are provided. Answers to the questions appear on pp. 92–95.

Context

- What has happened in Nigeria in the last hundred years or so?
- Why are there so many Christians in Nigeria?
- Why do most Nigerian authors write in English?
- What do 'colonialism' and 'postcolonial' mean?
- What is Adichie's background?
- Which writers influenced *Purple Hibiscus*?
- What is a hibiscus?

Nigeria – some history

Nigeria, a country in West Africa, is about the same size as Spain and Portugal. Do not confuse it with the similar-sized, separate, land-locked country, called 'Niger,' a former French colony, which lies immediately north of Nigeria.

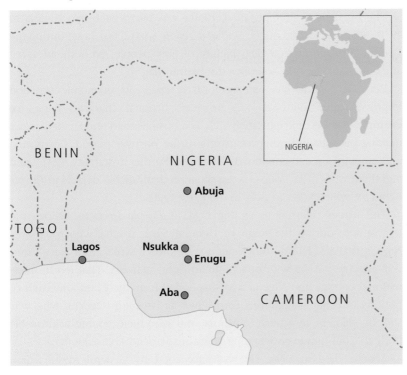

Nigeria and some of the places mentioned in the novel.

The British took control of the area they later called Nigeria during the late 1800s and early 1900s. Dame Flora Shaw, wife of Lord Lugard, suggested the name in 1897. The name was inspired by the 4,180-kilometre-long river

Niger, named by the Portuguese in the late Middle Ages when they first 'discovered' it. (They were the first Europeans to see it although, of course, Africans had known and used it for thousands of years.) The river has other names in African languages. 'Niger' is the Latin word for black and the name may refer to the local black-skinned population. Or it could be a corruption of an African word. No one is quite sure.

Nigeria remained a British colony until 1960, when it gained its independence, but the newly declared independent government was not stable. Years of being governed by a foreign power and long-standing tensions between regions made steady government difficult. A series of military take-overs known as 'coups' (pronounced 'coo' in the singular and 'coos' in the plural) followed, like the one that occurs in *Purple Hibiscus* (p. 24).

After two coups in 1966, the Igbo region of Nigeria tried to break away from the rest of the country by establishing an independent state called Biafra. This led to a bloody civil war between Nigeria and Biafra, referred to several times in *Purple Hibiscus* as history well within living memory (see p. 146, for example).

The breakaway attempt failed. Biafra was taken back into Nigeria in 1970. Adichie's second novel, *Half of a Yellow Sun* (2006), is set during the Biafran War and gives a clear picture of how people, on both sides, felt and suffered. The title describes the Biafran flag.

Because Nigeria has extensive oil reserves, its economic situation improved after the civil war. Adichie's fictional character Papa, for example, has become extremely rich as a businessman and factory owner making biscuits and other foodstuffs in the postwar period. Corruption and unemployment continued, however. Further instability developed and there were more coups — the situation that Adichie depicts in *Purple Hibiscus*, which is set loosely in the early 1990s.

The leader referred to as Big Oga in *Purple Hibiscus* echoes the atmosphere during the reign of General Sani Abacha who took over Nigeria in 1993. During this time, a well-known writer, Ken Saro-Wiwa, was executed along with other human rights activists. That led to international outrage and Nigeria was suspended from the Commonwealth of Nations. Adichie fictionalises Saro-Wiwa as Nwankiti Ogechi, who was shot by soldiers 'in a bush in Minna' and who then 'poured acid on his body to…kill him even when he was already dead' (pp. 200–01).

Abacha died in 1998. He was succeeded by General Abdul Salam Abubakar, who tried to restore order. Abubakar released political prisoners and held elections. General Olusegun Obasanjo, a former leader imprisoned during the rule of Abacha, was inaugurated as president of Nigeria in

1999. He was re-elected in 2003 followed by Umaru Yar'Adua in 2008 and Goodluck Jonathan in 2010. But corruption, tensions between factions and economic problems caused by falling oil prices are still going on.

Many readers of *Purple Hibiscus* have seen it as a small version, or mirror, of the situation in Nigeria as a whole. Kambili is strictly constrained by her family, just as every Nigerian is controlled by Big Oga, the despotic head of state.

Key quotation

They all told Papa to be careful. Stop going to work in your official car. Don't go to public places. Remember the bomb blast at the airport when a civil rights lawyer was traveling. Remember the one at the stadium during the pro-democracy meeting. Lock your doors. Remember the man shot in his bedroom by men wearing black masks.

(Kambili, p. 201)

Key quotation

'We are here to search your house. We're looking for documents designed to sabotage the peace of the university. We have information that you have been in collaboration with the radical student groups that staged the riots...' The voice sounded mechanical, the voice of a person reciting something written. The man speaking had tribal marks all over his cheek; there seemed to be no area of skin free of the ingrained lines.

(Kambili describing the raid on Ifeoma's flat by men from the 'special security unit', p. 230)

Text focus

Look carefully at the passage on pp. 24–25, from 'It was during family time...' (p. 24) to '...our economy was in a mess' (p. 25). Read it several times.

● Notice how Adichie focuses on the detail of what family members are doing. It is 'family time' — a chilling term for the limited, controlled timetabled slot each day when Kambili and Jaja are with both their parents. Adichie has Kambili recall the exact chess move (Papa had just checkmated Jaja) as they hear the announcement of the coup on the radio. She also describes exactly what they drank (mango juice). It creates an atmosphere in the room before Papa begins to talk, like a slow motion silent film. It is quite sinister.

● There is no direct speech in this passage. Everything Kambili recalls of what Papa says is in reported (or indirect) speech. It is implied ('but then most of what Papa said sounded important') that he often spoke in this way and that listening to him like this was habitual. The verb forms 'He liked', 'I would' and 'sometimes I wanted' reinforce the sense of continuousness.

- The relationship that Adichie depicts between Kambili and Papa is complex and even at this early point in the novel we see how deeply she loves him, listens closely to what he says and is moved by his physicality, especially his mouth with its 'rectangular lips'.
- Papa speaks emphatically (hence the repetition, the italics and the capital letters) of 'renewed democracy'. The child Kambili is impressed by his idealism. But there is also a sense here of the adult Kambili looking back ruefully to realise that Papa was not quite all he seemed and that, perhaps, it was just a grandiose way of speaking ('but then most of what Papa said sounded important)'.
- Look at the role that Adichie gives Papa's own newspaper, the *Standard*, in this passage. First, he goes out of the room to phone and the family know that he is giving instructions to his editor, Ade Coker. The next day, we learn that 'Only the *Standard* had a critical editorial, calling on the new military government to quickly implement a return to democracy plan.' This is compared with the opposite view expressed in *Nigeria Today* (a real newspaper, not fiction). Note that Papa has four copies of each paper delivered so that each family member can read his/her own.
- Study the beautiful simile in which Adichie has Kambili compare Papa's face with a coconut. It perfectly captures the image of his brown face and white teeth. It depicts a smile. Despite everything else that happens in this novel, this is a warm and loving image of a father from the point of view of an adoring, unquestioning child.

Nigerian culture and language

Nigeria consists of 36 states, of which Enugu (also the name of the state's capital city), where most of *Purple Hibiscus* is set, is one. Across these states, the country has over 250 ethnic groups. The three largest are the Igbo (or Ibo) in the east, the Hausa in the north and the Yoruba in the west.

About half the country is Muslim and about 40 per cent is Christian. Traditional religion, based on the worship of many gods and spirits, is still practised today, as Adichie shows us in the character of Papa-Nnukwu.

Kambili (pronounced 'Kam-bili', with the emphasis on the first syllable — see pp. 179–180) and her family are members of one of the largest ethnic groups in Nigeria, the Igbo. Igbo is, therefore, the family's ancestral language and Adichie often presents them speaking it.

English, however, became the official language of the country while it was a British colony, and it still is. This means, for example, that it is the language of government and education. Kambili and Jaja are being educated entirely in English, as their parents and Aunty Ifeoma were.

Papa-Nnukwu speaks only Igbo because he has not been to school or been taught to read and write.

Most Nigerians speak English and at least one African language. In *Purple Hibiscus*, characters move from one language to another continually. Adichie makes this clear by telling the reader which language is being spoken and peppering the text with Igbo words. His daughter Ifeoma and all the grandchildren use Igbo when they speak to Papa-Nnukwu, but English at school and often at home. By contrast, even though Papa grew up speaking Igbo and is fluent in it, it is unusual for him to use it other than to servants or the people on his country estate, and Adichie has Kambili comment on it when he does (see pp. 47 and 69, for example). He favours English as the 'civilised' language of white people and associates Igbo with the traditional 'heathen' Nigerian ways he loathes. He changes his accent — making it sound more British — when he is with the white Father Benedict or the white nuns who teach at Kambili's school (p. 46).

> **Key quotation**
>
> ...it was not just the figurines that came tumbling down, it was everything.
>
> (Kambili, p. 15)

Pause for thought

Chinua Achebe (Adichie's 'idol') neatly illustrates the conflicts between traditional Nigerian beliefs and 'modern' education in his short story 'Dead men's path'. Michael is the young black arrogant head of a village primary school trying — as Papa would in the same circumstances — to impose his version of European Christian education on the village elders.

Read this short story. Notice how much the priest has in common with Papa-Nnukwu. How many other parallels can you find between 'Dead men's path' and *Purple Hibiscus*?

> **Key quotation**
>
> 'You understand that it is wrong to take joy in pagan rituals, because it breaks the first commandment. Pagan rituals are... the gateway to Hell.'
>
> (Father Benedict at Kambili's confession, p. 106)

Christianity in Nigeria

European missionaries took Christianity to Nigeria. They tried to convert local people from their traditional religious practices to follow what they regarded as the 'true' religion. They ran schools for the children of converts and others, which meant they could ensure that children absorbed the Christian message while they were young and impressionable. Chinua Achebe describes this process and its effects in his famous 1958 novel *Things Fall Apart* in which Okonkwo, a strong traditional farmer, eventually loses everything. And there is a glimpse in *Purple Hibiscus* of how misguided missionary zeal could affect families when Papa-Nnukwu says, 'My son owns that house that can fit in every man in Abba, and yet many times I have nothing to put on my plate. I should not have let him follow those missionaries' (p. 83).

Nigerian women dancing outside a Catholic church in Enugu.

Barbara Davidson/Dallas Morning News/Corbis

Key quotation

'Is that so? Our own sons now go to be missionaries in the white man's land?...It is good my son. But you must never lie to them. Never teach them to disregard their fathers.'

(Papa-Nnukwu to Father Amadi, p. 172)

Kambili and her family are Catholics, and she and Jaja both attend Catholic schools run by monks and nuns under the ultimate leadership and guidance of the Pope in Rome. In 2005, there were an estimated 19 million baptised Catholics in Nigeria out of a population of around 150 million. Priests such as Adichie's fictional Father Benedict are white Europeans sent to Nigeria to run the churches.

In recent years, there has been a marked increase in young black Nigerians educated in Catholic schools who then decide to go into the priesthood. Father Amadi is one of these and, at the end of the novel, he is sent to do 'missionary' work in Europe. When he says to Papa-Nnukwu that he is going to be sent away, Papa-Nnukwu is much amused, seeing it as a neat bit of role reversal.

Traditionally the Catholic Church had strict ideas about sin and behaviour, although it is usually much gentler today. The kinder face of Catholicism is represented in the novel by Aunty Ifeoma and Father Amadi.

In *Purple Hibiscus*, Papa takes the hardest imaginable line with his children, seeing it as his responsibility to control rigidly everything they do and to punish them severely to save them from burning in Hell if they do not conform. 'That is what you do to yourself when you walk into sin. You burn your feet', he says, as he pours boiling water onto his daughter's bare feet (p. 194).

He is also adamant that his family should eat nothing before they take communion (holy bread and sometimes wine, which represent the body and blood of Christ), as we see when Kambili needs a painkiller just before the service but needs 'something in [her] stomach to hold the Panadol' (p. 101) and so eats some corn flakes (pp. 100–02). There is more about Papa's character and Catholicism in the *Characterisation* and *Themes* sections of this guide.

Colonialism

The British travelled the world extensively and took many lands as colonies from the sixteenth century onwards. These territories, known as the British Empire, included Australia, New Zealand, India, large parts of Africa (including Nigeria), many important islands (including Hong Kong, Malta and the Falklands), America (until 1776 when it declared independence after a war) and various other countries.

The colonies were important for one of two main reasons. Some had resources or valuable crops (such as the gold and diamonds in South Africa, or the sugar in the southern states of America) and cheap labour, which made Britain wealthy. Others were usefully positioned as military bases so that Britain could defend itself across the world. Malta, for example, played a vital part in the Second World War because of its Mediterranean position south of Italy and thousands of allied forces were based there, or passed through, between 1939 and 1945.

The British Empire was the largest empire the world has ever known but Britain was not the only European country to colonise other parts of the world. France, Belgium, Italy and Germany all had colonies in Africa. Spain, Portugal and Holland took colonies in other continents. Sometimes colonies were sold by one country to another (France sold Louisiana to America in 1803) or handed over as part of a treaty after a war (Britain got Gibraltar, previously Spanish, under the terms of the Treaty of Utrecht in 1713).

Few people questioned the morality of this. Rather, there was a sense that European colonisers were helping, for example Africans, to become more 'civilised' by giving them Christianity, grand buildings like the ones in nineteenth-century London or Paris, schools for their children and European laws. It was almost as if Europe thought it was grown up while Africa remained a child needing firm, top-down, guidance.

Grade *booster*

As you revise, note the number of times (with page numbers) Papa uses the words 'heathen', 'godless', 'pagan' or 'idol worshipper'. Use these references in essays when you are writing about Papa's extreme intolerance of his own background.

However, after the Second World War, British colonies began to seem an economic burden rather than an asset and most were granted independence — Nigeria in 1960, for example. This meant installing a government of local people who were then expected to run the country as a British-style democracy, with fair elections, well-organised parliaments and so on.

In fact, in Africa in particular, this has not usually worked. These new large countries with artificial boundaries fixed by the colonisers lack leaders who have the centuries of evolved experience that European governments have. The result is corruption and military coups, such as the one described in *Purple Hibiscus*.

That is why so many Africans are bitter about their colonial past. They argue that it was quite wrong of the British and other nations to plunder their countries for wealth, try to break up local culture and then leave them to flounder. Chinua Achebe, eminent Nigerian academic and author, puts it clearly:

> I will state simply my fundamental objection to colonial rule. In my view it is a gross crime for anyone to impose himself on another, to seize his land and his history and then to make out that the victim is some kind of ward or minor requiring protection.
>
> ('The Education of a British Protected Child', 1993, republished 2010 in a book of essays by Chinua Achebe with the same title, *The Education of a British Protected Child*)

A Nigerian such as the fictional Papa in *Purple Hibiscus*, desperate to be as 'British' as possible and to reject his ancestral culture, may be more unusual, but people like him do exist. He, too, is in a sense a victim of colonialism. He is not really British (other than technically as a citizen of a former colony, which entitles him to a British passport) and he is not fully African because he wants nothing to do with its way of doing things. That is part of the reason he is as he is — a tragic figure in many ways.

Pause for thought

Can colonialism ever be justified? Since it happened, how can, or should, former colonies now be supported? How do the events in *Purple Hibiscus* affect your views?

Grade *booster*

Make a point of carefully learning the spellings of unfamiliar African names (such as Papa-Nnukwu, Nsukka and Obiora) as you revise. An essay full of careless, avoidable spelling errors is unlikely to get a high grade.

Chimamanda Ngozi Adichie

Adichie was born in Nigeria in 1977 and was only 27 when *Purple Hibiscus* was first published in 2004. It has been a runaway, worldwide bestseller, republished many times and translated into other languages such as French, German, Spanish, Dutch and Hebrew. It was shortlisted for the Orange Prize in the UK and longlisted for the Man Booker Prize in 2004.

Adichie grew up on the campus of the University of Nigeria at Nsukka (where Aunty Ifeoma works and lives with her family in the novel). Both Adichie's parents worked for the university. Her father was a professor of statistics and her mother the university's first female registrar.

The fifth of six children, Adichie went to both primary and secondary school on the university campus (as Obiora, Amaka and Chima do in *Purple Hibiscus*). Then, aged 19, she joined her elder sister in America and went to universities there to do first a Bachelors degree and then a Masters in creative writing, having written stories for pleasure since childhood.

Chimamanda Ngozi Adichie.

Adichie was brought up in the Catholic faith, as Kambili, Jaja and their cousins are in the novel. But, quite unlike Kambili, no one forced her. Instead, in her teens, she took to Catholicism intensely from choice and did a lot of thinking and questioning, some of which is evident in *Purple Hibiscus*. Her understanding of the faith and people who hold to it underpins what happens in the novel too.

Educated in English and exposed mostly to British culture in school, it took Adichie a while to realise that she did not have to write about European things (of which she then had no experience) and that she was free to write about Nigeria, its people and history.

Her second major novel, *Half of a Yellow Sun*, was published in 2006 and won the Orange Broadband Prize for Fiction. It is set during the 1960s Nigerian Civil War.

When you are referring to the context of *Purple Hibiscus* in your essays, the examiners will want to see not only that you understand where the book is set and when but that you understand the importance of that background to the novel and how it supports Adichie's purpose. Use this table to give yourself a clearer idea of the difference between a higher- and foundation-tier answer to a question about Nigeria's role in the novel.

Grades A*–C points	Grades D–G points
Like almost all Nigerian writers, Adichie relates overall postcolonial experience to individual experience — Kambili and her family.	The novel is set in independent Nigeria.
Adichie fictionalises real events (death of Ken Saro-Wiwa and letter bomb to newspaper editor) to show how torn apart Nigeria is by this and other coups.	In the 1990s, there were a lot of troubles.
Adichie is part of the third generation of Nigerian writers helping readers to understand the impact of colonialism. Chinua Achebe, born 1930, and his contemporaries were the first.	Adichie is one of many Nigerian writers.
A novel about things falling apart, both politically and inside Kambili's family, and what happens to both is a direct result of the falling apart described in the nineteenth century of Chinua Achebe's 1958 novel *Things Fall Apart*.	Everything is breaking up.

Chinua Achebe and Nigerian literature

Since the country became independent, Nigeria has produced a steady stream of writers — novelists, poets and playwrights. Most of their work is, in some way, a response to the experience of Nigeria's having been taken over and ruled by the British for over 100 years and then set free to flounder. Critics call this body of work 'post-colonial literature' and Chimamanda Ngozi Adichie is part of it.

Nigeria's most famous postcolonial novelist (and poet and essayist) is Chinua Achebe, who was born in 1930 in the village of Ogidi, one of the first centres of Church of England missionary work in Nigeria. After the civil war, during which Achebe represented Biafra, he became Senior Research Fellow at the University of Nigeria, Nsukka, where Adichie grew up and where her fictional character in *Purple Hibiscus*, Aunty Ifeoma, works.

Achebe has lectured all over the world, received many international honours and is the author of over 20 books. His most famous title is the 1958 novel *Things Fall Apart*, which has sold over 10 million copies and been translated into more than 50 languages. The title comes from a poem by the Irish poet W. B. Yeats and refers here to the collapse of the traditional Igbo way of life when the missionaries arrived in West Africa in the nineteenth century. The novel is about Okonkwo, a tribesman of power and substance who sees the decay of everything he values, largely because of the arrival of white men with new laws and a new god.

Adichie is a passionate admirer of Chinua Achebe, old enough to be her grandfather, and boldly refers to his best-known novel in her opening sentence: 'Things started to fall apart at home when…' She discusses the influence Achebe has had on her writing in a talk you can watch at:

www.intelligencesquared.com/talks/chimamanda-ngozi-adichie-on-her-literary-influences-and-chinua-achebe.

Chinua Achebe.

'I wanted to write about colonialism, which I think every African writer does without meaning to' Adichie told a journalist in 2005. 'The way we are is very much the result of colonialism — the fact that I think in English, for example.' Other Nigerian authors who reflect the postcolonial experience in their work (and write in English) include:

- Wole Soyinka (born 1934). He has written poetry, plays, memoirs, novels and essays. He won the Nobel Prize for Literature in 1986. He has always been openly critical of Nigerian military dictators. You may be familiar with his poem 'The Telephone Conversation', which is included in many school anthologies.
- Buchi Emechta (born 1944). She writes plays, novels and short stories. Her most famous work is the novel *The Joys of Motherhood* (1979), which explores the experience of women in postcolonial Nigeria.

> **Pause for thought**
>
> How far do you think the domestic 'falling apart' which Adichie describes in Kambili's family is a small-scale reflection of the wider situation across Nigeria?

What does the title mean?

Hibiscus is a flowering shrub in the same family as hollyhocks and cotton. It grows throughout the world in warm-to-temperate, sub-tropical and tropical regions. The whole of Nigeria lies between the Tropic of Cancer and the Equator, which makes it an entirely tropical country. Hibiscus is common there.

The plant has large, showy flowers that are usually red, although some varieties come in white, pink, yellow and reddish orange. The purple hibiscus growing in Aunty Ifeoma's garden (p. 128) is unusual and Jaja comments on it. It is a new strain developed by Ifeoma's friend Phillipa, a university colleague in the botany (study of plants) department.

Later, Kambili and Jaja take some stems of purple hibiscus home and it is planted in the garden where years later it begins to flower (p. 9). There are far fewer purple flowers than red ones to start with, and purple hibiscus becomes a symbol of hope and change, which we will look at in more detail in the *Style* section.

A purple hibiscus plant in flower.

JAP_63/Fotolia

Review your learning

(Answers on p. 91)
1. When did Nigeria gain independence from Britain?
2. Who wrote the 1958 novel *Things Fall Apart*?
3. To which ethnic group in Nigeria do Kambili and her family belong?
4. Why did European countries want colonies elsewhere?
5. Why does English remain the official language of Nigeria?
6. Why are so many Nigerians (and other Africans) angry about their colonial past?

More interactive questions and answers online.

Plot and structure

- What happens in each section of *Purple Hibiscus?*
- What is the order of the events in the novel?
- How does the author organise her material?
- How does she keep the reader interested?

Plot

Breaking gods — Palm Sunday

- Jaja stands up to Papa for the first time.

In this short introductory section, Kambili, aged about 15, looks back from the future and describes the day when her elder brother Jaja defied their father, Papa, and refused to take the holy bread (or 'host' or 'wafer') from the priest, Father Benedict, during the solemn Palm Sunday church service. Back home and furious with his son, Papa throws his Catholic prayer book across the room in anger. It smashes Mama's china ornaments on a display stand ('étagère'). After a strained family lunch, Jaja walks assertively away to his room. Papa can, at this stage, do nothing about Jaja's defiance which, for Kambili, is 'fragrant with the undertones of freedom' (p. 16), like her aunt's unusual purple hibiscus.

> ### Key quotation
>
> **This had never happened before in my entire life, never.**
>
> (Kambili of Jaja's Palm Sunday defiance, p. 14)

> ### Pause for thought
>
> Mama says that the broken ornaments are not important (p. 10) but Kambili has noticed that her mother always polishes and rearranges them after violence from Papa and mentions this link several times during the novel. Can you explain the connection? Why will she now not need them (p. 15)?

Speaking with our spirits — Before Palm Sunday

- Military coup.
- Christmas at Abba.
- First visit to Aunty Ifeoma's flat.
- Papa-Nnukwu's death.
- Papa's punishment puts Kambili in hospital.
- Second visit to Aunty Ifeoma's flat.

Pages 19–26

The novel has now shifted back several years in time. The much younger Kambili, home for lunch after school, learns that her mother is pregnant. We see how close to Jaja she is. A military coup is declared, which distresses Papa.

Grade *booster*

Mama miscarries because Papa hits her. It happens again (p. 249). There was an earlier miscarriage six years earlier (p. 21) and Mama refers to 'the miscarriages' after Kambili's birth (p. 20). For a higher grade, note that Adichie — in an understated way — is telling you something deeply shocking about Papa's violence.

Pause for thought

Do parents have the right to apply this kind of pressure to children they want to do well academically? Whatever you think or feel about this, work out the reasons for your answer.

Pages 27–36

When the chauffeur, Kevin, drives Kambili and Jaja to school, they see soldiers and roadblocks but 'nothing changed at home'. One Sunday afternoon, Papa attacks Mama in their bedroom, because she felt sick in church and did not want to go visiting afterwards. It leads to an overnight stay in hospital and a miscarriage.

Pages 37–51

Ade Coker, editor of the newspaper that Papa owns, has been arrested for criticising the military dictatorship. Kambili has come second in her class at school, which leads to an uncomfortable interview with Papa who requires her to come first. At the beginning of the new term, he takes her to her Catholic school, run by nuns, and demands that she show him the girl she has to beat. Kambili clearly has no real friends at school.

Pages 52–70

It is Christmas and Kambili has come first at school. The family goes south to Abba where Papa and Mama originally came from. Papa owns a large house there and is a 'lord of the manor' figure to local people. There are many guests and meetings. Ade Coker, now released, and his family visit on their way to spend Christmas elsewhere. Kambili and Jaja are taken by Kevin to visit, briefly, their paternal grandfather, Papa-Nnukwu, whom Papa does not want to see (although he sends money via Kevin) because the old man will not convert to Christianity.

Pages 71–88

Ifeoma (Kambili's aunt and Papa's widowed sister) visits with her three children. Papa reluctantly agrees to let her take Kambili and Jaja out for the day. Unbeknown to Papa, Ifeoma collects her father, Papa-Nnukwu, and takes him on the trip too. Kambili worries because she knows how angry this would make Papa but is fascinated by Ifeoma's laughter and the confidence of her cousins.

Pages 89–109

After church on Christmas day, where Papa is treated like a respected and generous VIP, the family ceremonially greet the men and women of the umunna, or estate. Then Ifeoma and her children join Kambili's family for lunch. The next day, Sunday, Kambili takes a painkiller with a mouthful of cereal before church. Papa catches her and angrily 'punishes' Kambili, Jaja and Mama with his leather belt. Back in the city, all the family individually confess their sins to Father Benedict, after which it is agreed that Kambili and Jaja can go to Nsukka to stay with Ifeoma and her family in the university compound where she works as a lecturer. They set off in the car, driven by Kevin, with gas cylinders and sacks of food as gifts.

Pages 110–39

In Nsukka, Kambili finds Ifeoma's flat and way of life basic and cramped compared with what she is used to. There is little money and often no fuel or water to flush the lavatory but the family is cheerful, united and happy. They practise a much kinder, more tolerant form of Catholicism than Papa's, although her cousin Amaka is bitter towards Kambili. Ifeoma shows the visitors around the campus, where conditions have seriously deteriorated since the military coup. Later, back at the flat, Ifeoma's priest, Father Amadi, comes to supper. Kambili is secretly impressed because he is young, black, pleasant and approachable. He is at ease with the family and they with him.

Pages 140–61

Kambili overhears Amaka's suggestion that she and Jaja are 'abnormal' because they find it so difficult to relate to others. Chima notices Jaja's deformed finger and Kambili recalls its deliberate mutilation by Papa as a punishment when Jaja was ten. Mama phones and reports that the offices of Papa's newspaper have been brutally raided and Ade Coker arrested again. Clearly worried, Papa phones later and asks Ifeoma to keep the children for a few days longer. Ifeoma learns that Papa-Nnukwu is ill and, with Father Amadi's help, arranges to bring him to Nsukka.

Grade *focus*

When you are referring to the context of *Purple Hibiscus* in your essays, the examiners will want to see that you understand not only the story itself but how it is organised. Use this table to give yourself a clearer idea of the difference between a higher- and foundation-tier answer to a question about how Adichie tells her story.

Grades A*–C points	Grades D–G points
Palm Sunday is the day in Kambili's narrative when everything changed, which is why she structures the story around it.	Kambili remembers Palm Sunday.
By starting three quarters of the way through the story, Kambili stresses the pivotal nature of Palm Sunday.	Most of the story is a flashback.
The length of each part of the novel is significant too. The novel is framed by two short parts, like a prologue and an epilogue. Most of the story lies in the long part entitled 'Speaking with our spirits — Before Palm Sunday', which leads up to Palm Sunday (pp. 17–253). Adichie is showing the reader just how deeply conditioned Kambili is before Jaja's defiance.	The parts of the novel are different lengths.

Pages 162–205

Kambili witnesses Papa-Nnukwu's morning prayers and is astonished by their similarity to the Christian prayers. Father Amadi takes Kambili to the football stadium. A bond is forming between them as Kambili feels the beginning of physical attraction to a man, although she does not understand her own feelings. He tries to persuade her to be more casual and natural by playing volleyball with him. Then she watches, holding his pullover, while he plays football with a group of poor boys. Later, Ifeoma tells her that Papa has found out that his children are staying in the same flat as their 'heathen' grandfather, Papa-Nnukwu, and wants them home. That night, Papa-Nnukwu dies in his sleep. When Papa arrives to collect Kambili and Jaja, he is furious that his sister did not summon a Catholic priest to the dying old man.

Home in Enugu, Jaja asks his father for the key to his own bedroom so that he can have some privacy. That, and their not having told him that Papa-Nnukwu was also staying at Ifeoma's, leads to Papa's pouring boiling water over his children's bare feet as a punishment.

The perpetrators of the coup continue to commit atrocities and Nigeria is suspended from the Commonwealth.

Pages 206–16

Ade Coker is killed by a letter bomb sent by the government. Papa is devastated and distracted. When he discovers the painting of Papa-Nnukwu, brought home from Nsukka, he beats Kambili so badly that she wakes in hospital and takes weeks to recover. Visiting her hospitalised niece with Father Amadi, Ifeoma tells Mama that she and the children should stay with her in Nsukka at least until Easter.

Pages 217–39

Kambili convalesces at Ifeoma's flat with Jaja. The university is now run by a 'single administrator' (a government-appointed dictator). Forthright, Ifeoma thinks she will soon lose her job. There is a student riot against the single administrator and Ifeoma's flat is raided because she is suspected of encouraging the students. She considers moving to America. Meanwhile, for the family meal, Jaja kills a chicken brought by a student who is giving up education and Kambili is taken to the market by Father Amadi to have her hair plaited.

Pages 240–53

Kambili and Jaja go to church with Ifeoma's family and find the service, led by Father Amadi, more relaxed than they are used to. Mama arrives unexpectedly by taxi and reveals that Papa has hit her so hard that, six weeks pregnant, she has miscarried yet again. Mama stays the night but insists that she and her children return to Enugu when Papa, 'who has not been well' with 'migraines and fever', picks them up the next day. Then comes Palm Sunday, where the novel opened.

The pieces of gods — After Palm Sunday

- Third visit to Aunty Ifeoma's flat.
- Papa murdered by Mama.
- Jaja confesses.

Pages 257–70

Everything seems to have changed. Papa is quite ill — skin trouble, shaking hands. On Good Friday, Ifeoma rings to say she has been sacked. Jaja announces, with new-found assertiveness, that he and Kambili are returning to Nsukka for Easter. They arrive there to find that Ifeoma is arranging for the move to America and Father Amadi is to be transferred by the Church to Germany.

Pages 271–87

Ifeoma takes the children to Akope, where Kambili believes she has a religious vision. Ifeoma is granted a visa to emigrate to America with her children. Father Amadi says goodbye to people on the campus and there are tender leave-taking moments between him and Kambili.

A phone call from Mama announces Papa's death.

Pages 288–91

Pause for thought

In what ways are the police at fault here? What questions should they have asked Jaja and others before arresting him?

Mama tells Kambili and Jaja that she killed Papa by poisoning his tea. An autopsy indicates death by poisoning. When the police come, Jaja (who was not in Enugu at the time) confesses and is arrested.

A different silence — The present

- Kambili and Mama visit Jaja in prison.
- After almost three years, his release is secured.

Kambili and her mother have been visiting Jaja in prison for nearly three years. Now the military dictator is dead and they have bribed lawyers and others to get Jaja freed next week.

Ifeoma and her children are thriving in America. Kambili plans to visit them soon with Jaja and her mother. She hears regularly from Father Amadi, who continues to remind her that she is valued.

Key quotation

'See, the purple hibiscuses are about to bloom,' Jaja said, as we got out of the car.

(Kambili reporting Jaja's comment, p. 253).

Key quotation

There is so much that is still silent between Jaja and me. Perhaps we will talk more with time, or perhaps we never will be able to say it all, to clothe things in words, things that have long been naked.

(Kambili, p. 306)

Text focus

Look at the passage that begins 'Rain splashed across the floor…' on p. 217 and ends with '…my fingers and eating it' on p. 218.

- Kambili has just been discharged from a long stint in hospital after being seriously injured ('I had nearly died') by her father. This passage depicts a scene of contented domestic calm in Ifeoma's flat where Kambili has been sent to convalesce.
- The weather — which mirrors Kambili's strange mood — is undecided. It is raining in strong sunshine, the 'raindrops glinting with sunlight'. She remembers her mother's referring to God's indecision. Maybe God is deciding now about her future.

- Her cousins are treating her gently because they know she has been seriously ill. Obiora has helped her into the flat earlier while Chima carried her bag. Now Obiora offers her a mango.
- Because it is so quiet, Kambili notices small sounds that would normally be lost, such as Obiora's pounding his mango to pulp (which carries a faint echo of Kambili's injuries).
- She also notices fresh smells such as the 'edible scent' of the wet soil, which may be a symbol of a new beginning for her. Wet soil allows growth and development. Perhaps Kambili can grow and develop too.
- Jaja is outside kneeling and she imagines joining him and tasting the soil, having dug it out in a clump with her fingers.
- This is a sensuous passage in which all Kambili's senses are heightened. In just a few lines, she uses sight, hearing, smell, taste and touch.
- The inclusion of a solemn but thoughtful interlude passage like this here is part of the rhythm of Adichie's storytelling. The reader has just come from the horror of Kambili's deliberately inflicted injuries and long stay in hospital, and the passage is followed by the local children's noisy excitement at catching the *aku*, flying insects, driven up by the rain.

Structure

The novel's shape

Adichie's story is told by her narrator, Kambili, in four parts of varied length. The first, 'Breaking gods — Palm Sunday' (pp. 1–16), and the last, 'A different silence — The present' (pp. 293–307), are short and act as a frame around the main part of the story. We could call them the novel's prologue and epilogue.

Most of the story is told in the long part entitled 'Speaking with our spirits — Before Palm Sunday' (pp. 17–253) and the shorter one entitled 'The pieces of gods — After Palm Sunday' (pp. 255–91).

Adichie has chosen not to divide *Purple Hibiscus* into the traditional numbered chapters (which in some books in the past each had their own title too), but she does lay her book out in sections which are effectively chapters — 12 in the novel's long second part and three in the third, shorter part which follows it. Occasionally there is also a break within these sections (pp. 166 and 246, for example) when she wants to build in a slight pause or change of direction. The novel's pattern looks like this:

Timeline

1994	Spring	Jaja says Mama's baby due October (p. 23)	
		Coup. Military dictatorship (p. 24)	
	Few weeks later	Mama miscarries (p. 34)	
	End of school term	Ade Coker arrested (p. 37)	
		Kambili 'only' 2nd in school exams (p. 39)	
	New term	Kambili to school with Papa (p. 46)	
	Christmas holiday	Kambili has come first at school (p. 52)	
		Family to Abba, where children visit Papa-Nnukwu and meet Ifeoma and family (pp. 53–103)	
1995	After New Year	Back to Enugu	
	6 January	Epiphany, mass, confession	
	7 January	Kambili and Jaja to Nsukka (first visit)	
		Meet Father Amadi. Papa Nnukwu joins them and dies (pp. 110–90)	
	About 14 January	Home to Enugu. Jaja asks for room key. Papa scalds both children's feet to punish them (pp. 192–97)	
	Later that term	Ade Coker killed (p. 206)	
		Papa beats Kambili and she spends weeks in hospital (pp. 209–16)	
	Not long before Easter	Kambili to Nsukka to convalesce with Ifeoma's family and Jaja	During this time, back in Enugu, Mama is starting to poison Papa's tea (p. 290)
		Stay is extended because of political problems in city (pp. 216–53)	
	Friday before Palm Sunday	Mama arrives in Nsukka, having had yet another miscarriage caused by Papa's violence (p. 247)	
	Saturday before Palm Sunday	Mama takes Kambili and Jaja home to Enugu (p. 252)	

NOVEL STARTS HERE	Palm Sunday	Jaja refused to take communion. Papa throws prayer book and breaks Mama's ornaments (p. 3 and p. 253)	
	Good Friday	Ifeoma phones with news of sacking. Jaja insists he and Kambili return to Nsukka for Easter (pp. 260–61)	
	Week or two after Easter	News of Papa's death (p. 286) Return to Enugu (p. 288) Mama confesses to poisoning (p. 290) Jaja arrrested (p. 291)	
	NEARLY THREE YEARS PASS		
1998	Spring	Jaja's imminent release from prison following death of 'Big Oga' and a new, more democratic government (pp. 295–97)	
NOVEL ENDS HERE			

Note: Adichie is not specific about dates. Her novel is set in the mid-1990s. This timeline assumes that Adichie's 'Big Oga' is based on General Sani Abacha. He seized power and suppressed opposition in 1993 and died in 1998 of a 'sudden heart attack', although there were rumours similar to the ones that Adichie applies to her fictional Head of State on pp. 296–97.

The effect of this arrangement is to make the novel feel enclosed rather than using chapters that might open it out. And it works well because almost all the action of the novel takes place in Kambili's family homes in Enugu and Abba and at Ifeoma's home in Nsukka. Kambili's horizons are limited and narrow and this is reflected in the tight structure of the novel.

The flashback

The plot of *Purple Hibiscus* is not revealed in the order in which it happened. The novel opens with the events of Palm Sunday (the Sunday before Easter on which Christians remember Jesus riding into Jerusalem on a donkey over palm leaves thrown down by the crowd). These events actually happen more than a year after the beginning of the main action. So most of the novel is a flashback which catches up with itself on p. 253.

The centre of the novel is Palm Sunday. What happens then is a turning point. Everything changes. Jaja openly defies Papa who is, for the first time, powerless to combat his son's assertiveness. When Jaja leaves the dining table without permission (p. 14), there is nothing his father can do about it and Kambili's sense of everything falling apart is stronger than ever.

Recurring ideas in the structure

Adichie uses her 14-page opening section to introduce most of the issues that the novel is concerned with.

Papa's religious devotion and his contrasting violence

We are aware of Papa's violence from his hurling of the missal (a Catholic prayer book) in the very first sentence, and it is immediately contrasted with his religious devotion — the image of him firmly marking with ash the faces of worshippers on Ash Wednesday. Papa is a man of strange contrasts and contradictions and the reader knows this from the first page.

The figurines

Mama's fragile ornaments on the étagère are smashed on the first page by the hurled book. These expensive 'figurines' are china ballet dancers (see p. 35). They are European fine art and are displayed on a showy piece of French-style furniture with glass shelves: the étagère. They

Pause for thought

How much difference do you think it would have made to the effect of *Purple Hibiscus* if Adichie had used numbered and/or titled chapters?

Pause for thought

What do you think *Purple Hibiscus* would have lost (or gained) as a novel if Adichie had placed events in chronological order – starting when she hears of her mother's pregnancy and without the flashback?

Grade *booster*

To write confidently about *Purple Hibiscus*, and therefore raise your grade, you need a clear understanding of events in the Church calendar that Adichie mentions because they are part of the structure of the novel:

- Ash Wednesday: 40 days before Easter
- Palm Sunday: one week before Easter
- Good Friday: between Palm Sunday and Easter Sunday
- Easter Sunday: date varies from mid-March to mid-April
- Epiphany: 6 January
- Christmas: 25 December

are part of the way in which Kambili's family, at her father's insistence, try to distance themselves from their African heritage and value only British and European traditions and ideas.

Kambili has gradually come to understand that cleaning and looking after the figurines were her mother's way of calming herself whenever Papa has hit her — a sort of silent therapy (see pp. 35 and 192–93 for examples). Notice, too, that these ornaments are delicate and break easily. By linking the figurines with Mama's gentle, inadequate attempts to cope with the violence she lives with, Adichie is comparing the fragility of the broken ornaments with the eventual failure (breaking down) of Mama's passivity. The breaking of the figurines — no longer needed — in a sense justifies her decision to poison Papa.

Key quotation

I used to wonder why she polished [the figurines] each time I heard the sounds from their room, like something being banged against the door. Her rubber slippers never made a sound on the stairs, but I knew she went downstairs when I heard the dining room door open. I would go down to see her standing by the étagère with a kitchen towel soaked in soapy water.

(Kambili, p. 10)

Key quotation

The last time, only two weeks ago, when her swollen eye was still the black-purple color of an overripe avocado, she had rearranged them after she polished them.

(Kambili, pp. 10–11)

Now, on Palm Sunday, she tells Kambili that she will not replace the broken ornaments (p. 15). We discover, 275 pages later on (p. 290), but only a few days later in the novel's time frame, that Mama has already started to poison Papa at this point. '…it was not just the figurines that came tumbling down, it was everything' Adichie has Kambili say (p. 15), looking back on the events of Palm Sunday. Mama will no longer need her figurines.

The hibiscuses

Another idea that runs through the novel, first introduced in the short opening section, is that of hibiscuses changing colour as a reflection of the changes in Kambili's family and in Nigeria. As a trigger to move back in time to life before the first visit to Nsukka, she refers to the time 'when all the hibiscuses in our front yard were a startling red' (p. 16) — that is, before there were any signs that things would fall apart. Adichie uses this as a linking device to hold her novel together — it is part of its structure. The role of the hibiscus as a symbol will be further considered in the *Style* section.

Use of structure to introduce characters

Characters are, of course, central to any novel. In the opening part of *Purple Hibiscus*, Adichie introduces four main ones and Sisi, the servant. As well as Papa, we meet Mama, Jaja and Kambili herself. The *Characterisation* section provides more details but for now, in terms of the novel's structure, notice how Adichie shows the most important aspects of these characters in the first 14 pages of her novel, before she doubles back to explain what has led up to Palm Sunday.

We see Jaja, 17, being defiant. In the next part of the novel, we find out what had happened to Jaja and what he had learned — especially in Nsukka with Ifeoma's family — to bring him to this point. This standing up for what he now believes is right is also linked with his behaviour at the end of the novel in taking responsibility for his father's actions by going to prison for a crime he has not committed.

Then there is Mama, recently beaten by Papa yet again and limping, having endured yet another miscarriage as the novel opens. She seems meek but something is changing. We are then shown why and how Mama is as she is.

Obedient, frightened Kambili, 15, is astonished by Jaja's behaviour but she begins to see it as 'rare, fragrant with the undertones of freedom', like 'Aunty Ifeoma's experimental purple hibiscus'.

Hooking the reader

The structuring of Adichie's opening sentence and of her 14-page opening section is a device to catch the reader's attention. The hints are tantalising. If things have 'started to fall apart at home', what were they like before? Why is Papa so violent and dictatorial and yet so pious and the winner of a human rights award? Why is Mama so stoical and no longer in need of her ballet-dancing figurines? It is quite a successful way to draw in the intrigued reader who wants answers to these, and other, questions.

Subplots

The main plot in *Purple Hibiscus* is about Kambili's immediate family and the complex relationship between the four of them, which leads, eventually, to Papa's poisoning by Mama and Jaja's imprisonment. Think of this as the novel's backbone.

From this main story line, however, hang several smaller stories or subplots. They are closely linked to the main narrative but they could be told as separate stories independent of the main plot. This is part of the way Adichie has structured her novel. The subplots in *Purple Hibiscus* include:

- Ade Coker: his radical editing of the *Standard*, his death and the plight of his bereaved family.
- Aunty Ifeoma's family: her widowhood, job, relationship with her children and their new life in the USA.
- Kambili's friendship with Father Amadi: her love for him, his nurturing of a damaged teenager, his departure to Germany and letters.

The subplots are there to tell, or show, the reader more about the main plot — to deepen it. For example, Adichie shows us how Kambili's thoughts and feelings at home begin to change after she has met Father Amadi. Because Ifeoma is the relatively liberated, outward-looking working woman she is, she can see that Kambili, Jaja and their mother have to, somehow, extricate themselves from her brother. Finally, we learn more about Papa from his attitude to Ade Coker's family.

Review your learning

(Answers on p. 91)

1. What happened on Palm Sunday?
2. Where, and from whom, do Kambili and Jaja begin to learn that their father's way is not the only way of living?
3. How many parts is *Purple Hibiscus* divided into?
4. Where do the events of the novel begin?
5. What do you learn about Papa in the first two pages?
6. What is the significance of the figurines on the étagère?

More interactive questions and answers online.

Characterisation

- Who are the characters?
- What are they like?
- How does Chimamanda Ngozi Adichie present them?
- How do the characters relate to each other?
- How do they fit into the novel's themes and ideas?

In this chapter, we examine the characters of *Purple Hibiscus* and the ways in which Adichie presents, develops and uses them. The next two chapters are about themes and Adichie's style. Of course, these three topics are closely linked. Like all authors, Adichie uses characters to explore her themes, and her style underpins everything. Be aware of this overlap as you revise.

Papa

Papa says

- 'You cannot stop receiving the body of our Lord. It is death, you know that.' (p. 6)
- 'You didn't put in your best this term. You came second because you chose to.' (pp. 41–42)
- '"Why do you walk into sin?" [...] "Why do you like sin?"' (p. 102)
- 'This is what you do to yourself when you walk into sin. You burn your feet.' (p. 194)
- 'Everything I do for you, I do for your own good.' (p. 196)
- '"I should have made Ade hold that story [...]. I should have protected him. I should have made him stop that story."' (p. 207)

Papa

- is the central, dominant figure in Kambili's narrative
- is an educated man who has studied in Britain
- throws a book at his son when he realises that Jaja is rebelling

---

Key quotation

[Aunty Ifeoma] said once that Papa was too much of a colonial product. She had said this in a mild, forgiving way, as if it were not Papa's fault, as one would talk about a person who was shouting gibberish from a severe case of malaria.

(Kambili, p. 13)

- refuses to see his idol-worshipping father but sends him small sums of money
- is often tender and loving with his children
- disapproves of his sister and her children
- causes his wife to have several miscarriages by hitting her
- pours boiling water on his children's feet to punish them
- almost kills Kambili when he discovers she has disobeyed him
- gives large sums of money to the church and the poor (pp. 44 and 54), including half his fortune when he dies
- criticises the military coup through his newspaper
- is poisoned by his wife

> **Key quotation**
>
> **He lowered the kettle into the tub, tilted it toward my feet. He poured the hot water on my feet, slowly, as if he were conducting an experiment and wanted to see what would happen.**
>
> (Kambili, p. 194)

Papa thinks that

- his strict view of Roman Catholicism is the only way to live
- Nigerian traditionalists (like his father), who worship idols, will go to hell
- he must punish his wife and children severely if they stray in the smallest way from his instructions
- governments should be democratically elected
- 'godless' coups are disastrous for the people of Nigeria
- rich people should give generously to the less well-off, as he does (Christian charity)

> **Key quotation**
>
> **'Eugene quarrels with the truths that he does not like.'**
>
> (Ifeoma to Mama, p. 95)

> **Key quotation**
>
> **'Do you know that Eugene pays the school fees of up to a hundred of our people? Do you know how many people are alive because of your brother?'** (Mama to Ifeoma, p. 250)

Adichie presents Papa

- entirely through Kambili's narrative
- as a complex man of many parts — kind, tender and generous but also violent, volatile and uncompromising
- as a commentary on the political situation in Nigeria in the mid-1990s

> **Key quotation**
>
> **'Uncle Eugene is not a bad man, really [...]. People have problems, people make mistakes.'**
>
> (Amaka, p. 251)

Conclusions

Eugene Achike, or Papa, does many cruel things, such as rejecting his father, hitting his wife so often and so hard that several pregnancies end in miscarriage and ruthlessly punishing his children by, for example attacking them with a belt (p. 102) and burning their feet (pp. 194–95). He does not help his sister, Ifeoma, who is so clearly in need, although she jokes bitterly about his having offered her help when her husband died provided that she dressed and behaved exactly as her brother ordered (p. 95). Nonetheless, Papa is not simply a fairy-tale monster set up for the reader to hate.

Adichie's subtle characterisation ensures that we also see Papa giving money to the poor and to his church (pp. 5, 90, 297) and frequently has Kambili describe an affectionate loving relationship with her father (pp. 8 and 41). She also shows Papa working behind the scenes — in a way his daughter is only loosely aware of but the reader is meant to notice — to maintain a momentum of objection to the military coup (first mentioned on p. 24). This leads, eventually, to the murder of the *Standard*'s editor Ade Coker (p. 206), about which Papa feels deep remorse and does all he can to help Coker's widow and children.

It is after the attack on Kambili (which puts her, badly injured, in hospital) that Mama finally realises that this situation cannot go on. She poisons Papa's tea (p. 290) over several weeks and he is already ill with the effects of it on Palm Sunday as the novel opens (p. 6).

Papa behaves as he does partly because he genuinely believes — or has convinced himself — that this is what the Roman Catholic faith requires. And he claims to admire democracy and European ways. In fact, Adichie makes it clear that, although he does not realise it, his dictatorial behaviour at home is much like that of the African dictators. He is an extremist. And he has a controlling personality.

He is also a man who struggles hard against his own shortcomings. He talks a great deal about sin. In the Catholic Church, sins such as pride, greed and anger are taken seriously and Papa often lectures his children about them. And they have to confess their sins regularly to the priest (p. 105).

As Kambili describes what he says and does, Adichie makes her unaware of her father's sinning, although the reader can see past her narration. For example, Papa is evidently quite greedy with a fat stomach and bottom (pp. 41 and 101). Also, in spite of himself, he is proud of his achievements and behaves ostentatiously in church (pp. 4–5). And when he attacks Kambili after discovering that she has a drawing of her deceased heathen grandfather, he becomes angry and 'out of control' (p. 210) as he kicks her and talks continually 'in a mix of Igbo and English'. Thus, Papa condemns roundly in his children the urges he cannot control in himself. Adichie observes and depicts this complex mindset precisely and convincingly.

Pause for thought

Papa's near-fatal attack on Kambili (pp. 210–11) happens just after the murder of Ade Coker and Papa's great guilt. Can you work out a connection?

Pause for thought

Which do you find the more disturbing: Papa's planned, careful scalding of Kambili's feet (pp. 194–95) or the angry kicking which puts her in hospital (pp. 210–11)? Why?

Grade *booster*

You will get a higher grade for an exam answer which shows that you understand that Papa is presented as a complex man of contradictions, than if you discuss him as if he were a wicked ogre in a fairy story.

Grade *focus*

When you are writing about the character of Papa, the examiners will want to see that you understand how complex he is. Use this table to give yourself a clearer idea of the difference between a higher- and foundation-tier answer to a question about Papa.

Grades A*–C points	Grades D–G points
Strict and misguided, but sincere interpretation of his Roman Catholic Christianity leads Papa to some cruel actions, such as burning Kambili's and Jaja's feet to punish them.	Papa is a cruel man who burns his children's feet.
Papa works hard to promote democracy and condemn military dictatorship, but he makes a major error of judgement leading to Ade Coker's murder.	Papa lets Ade Coker get killed.
As a rich man, Papa regards it as his Christian duty to help others with money. He pays for many things at his churches in Enugu and Abba, gives money away and supports 'his' people by paying, for example, school fees, but he does not help the poor members of his own family — his father and sister whose views differ from his own — so that his understanding of the Christian ethic is shown to be narrow and limited.	Papa leaves half his money to the church, not to his family.
Papa totally rejects the traditional 'idol worship' of his ancestors and will not see his own father who refuses to convert to Christianity. He genuinely believes that anyone who is not a Christian will burn in hell.	Papa won't visit his father.

Kambili

Kambili says

- 'I wanted to stay like that forever, listening to his voice, to the important things he said. It was the same way I felt when he smiled, his face breaking open like a coconut with the brilliant white meat inside.' (p. 25)
- 'I had never seen anyone undress; it was sinful to look upon another person's nakedness.' (p. 117)
- 'I had never thought about the university, where I would go or what I would study. When the time came, Papa would decide.' (p. 130)

- 'I could not reconcile the blond Christ hanging on the burnished cross in St. Agnes and the sting-scarred legs of those boys.' (p. 178)
- 'The pain of contact was so pure, so scalding, I felt nothing for a second. And then I screamed.' (p. 194)
- 'His body touching mine was tense and delicious.' (p. 221)
- 'Everything came tumbling down after Palm Sunday.' (p. 257)
- 'We will take Jaja to Nsukka first, and then we'll go to America to visit Aunty Ifeoma […] and Jaja will plant purple hibiscus.' (pp. 306–07)

Text focus

Read the whole of p. 51 carefully several times.
- Kambili is at school with contemporaries, away from family. Adichie rarely presents Kambili in such a situation, which for any other teenager (Amaka, for example) would be quite normal.
- Adichie makes sure we see 'past' what Kambili is 'telling' us. Ezinne, Chinwe and the other girls have mistaken Kambili's intense nervousness and fear, because of what is going on at home, for standoffishness. Kambili is frightened that if she keeps Kevin, the chauffeur, waiting she will be punished at home. Her father once slapped the sides of her face hard because she was a few minutes late coming out of school — yet another example of Papa's unreasonable strictness and violence.
- Kambili speaks to Ezinne only in short, rather abrupt sentences. She is unable to hold a conventional conversation with her.
- Adichie's presentation of Ezinne makes it clear that the girl is trying to be kind to Kambili by acting as an intermediary between her and Chinwe. She offers advice: 'Maybe you should try and talk to her.' She is also perceptive and has a sense that all is not as it seems with Kambili: 'I'm not saying you feel too big. I am saying that is what Chinwe and most of the girls think.'
- Even as Kambili, who would clearly like to be friends with the other girls, makes a fumbling excuse for running away quickly at the end of the school day, she thinks about lying and wondering whether she will need to confess it formally as a sin. Adichie wants us to see that Kambili is so deeply conditioned by her upbringing that she is quite unable to think for herself.
- This passage is a good illustration of the gulf between Kambili and normal life. Compare it with page 141 when Kambili is unable to chat and act naturally with Amaka's friends, much as she would like to.
- Adichie makes it clear here that Kambili is at a rather exclusive school for which well-off parents pay high fees. Chinwe's father is as rich as Kambili's. Ezinne is trying to tell her that she has a lot in common with Chinwe — all she has to do is relax and talk to her. Kambili is prevented from doing that by all the stresses and fears which are hidden inside her.

Kambili

- narrates the story
- before Palm Sunday meekly obeys her father in everything
- hero-worships her charismatic father
- is conditioned to an extreme form of Roman Catholicism
- is frequently physically punished/abused by her father
- is deeply troubled by her mother's plight
- begins to realise that there are other ways of living through observing her aunt and cousins
- has no friends until she meets Father Amadi and gets to know her cousins better
- becomes attached to Father Amadi
- supports her mother after Papa's death and during Jaja's imprisonment
- mourns her father in spite of everything

> **Key quotation**
>
> I wanted to say I was sorry, that I did not want her to dislike us for not watching satellite. I wanted to tell her that although huge satellite dishes lounged on top of the houses in Enugu and here, we did not watch TV. Papa did not pencil in TV time on our schedules.
>
> (Kambili, p. 79)

Adichie presents Kambili

- as an intelligent, studious 15-year-old
- as a child who is cowed by her father without fully realising it, so the novel shows her growing towards independent thought
- as a loving daughter and sister to Mama and Jaja
- as an adolescent who is developing normal adult feelings and urges
- as the victim of what in the twenty-first-century developed world would be called 'domestic abuse'
- as a commentator on the behaviour of others in the novel and of the wider situation in Nigeria

> **Pause for thought**
>
> Kambili is subjected to dreadful punishments by her dictatorial father, yet she loves him deeply and tenderly. How do you explain this?

> Grade **booster**
>
> To attract the highest marks, make detailed reference in your essays to Adichie's presentation of Kambili rather than writing descriptively about Kambili's character as if she were someone you know.

Conclusions

Although Kambili is 15, has an adult body (she has periods, p. 100; Ifeoma teases her about her breasts, p. 72) and Papa-Nnukwu comments that she is nearly ready for a suitor (p. 64), she is very much a child at the beginning of the novel. This is partly because she has no friends and is not allowed to think for herself. She is not growing up normally. 'Are you sure they're not abnormal, Mom?' Kambili overhears Amaka ask Ifeoma (p. 141), having observed that her cousin cannot communicate with and relate to girls her own age.

Every minute of Kambili's life (and Jaja's) is controlled by Papa, who writes detailed timetables for his children to include study time, prayer, siesta, eating, sleeping and so on (p. 24). Aunty Ifeoma's astonishment at this, and the way she confiscates the schedules while Kambili and Jaja are staying with her, reminds the reader just what an extraordinary way of bringing up children this is (p. 124).

Kambili is serious and solemn. She believes everything her father tells her while at the same time knowing that things in her own home are not quite right. For example, she implicitly agrees with Jaja when he says that they will protect the new baby from its father (p. 23). She is astonished to hear Ifeoma and her family praying for the blessing of laughter (p. 127). Father Amadi remarks that he has not seen Kambili laugh or smile (p. 139). Ifeoma tactfully says that her niece is shy. Actually she is repressed, deeply damaged and paralysed by a feeling she does not seem to recognise as fear.

She develops a passion for Father Amadi because he is kind and gentle to her and takes a personal interest. Kambili is, without understanding why she feels as she does, sexually drawn to his pleasant manliness. This, of course, can never be properly reciprocated because Father Amadi is a Catholic priest, which means he has to be celibate.

Kambili changes and develops during the novel. Although it is Jaja who rebels on Palm Sunday, it is Kambili's inner thoughts and observations that Adichie shares with the reader. Kambili is utterly astounded but she learns, on Palm Sunday, that if Jaja makes a strong stand there is nothing Papa can do about it. She and her brother, she realises, could think for themselves as Ifeoma's children do. But it goes wrong of course because Jaja goes to prison after Papa's death and Kambili has to look after her damaged mother. No more studying, schedules or dreadful punishments for disobedience; instead, the two disturbed women (Kambili is suddenly no longer a child) have to take charge of their own lives and work to get Jaja released from prison.

Pause for thought

After Papa's death, Kambili feels a mixture of 'shame and grief' and 'so many other things that I cannot name' (p. 305). What do you think these other feelings might be? Relief? Regret? Anger?

Text focus

Read from 'Then I heard Papa's raised voice…' on p. 69 to the end of the section on p. 70.

- This is a dramatic passage that relies on dialogue and the movement of people for its impact. To feel its full effect, try acting it out in a group as a mini-playlet.

- Papa is angry with an 'enraged timber' in his voice. He is also out of control and 'screaming'. Anger or wrath is a major sin for Catholics but here is Papa giving in to it. There is no Christian forgiveness for, or kindness toward, the old man, Anikwenwa. So Adichie is using this situation to develop her characterisation of Papa as an intolerant bigot and a man who is afraid of losing the upper hand.
- Adichie's sketching in of the details, such as 'wrinkled old man', 'torn white singlet' and 'unsteady gait' — indicators of age and poverty — helps to show how harmless the visitor is.
- Papa utters the words 'my house' six times. It is proprietorial, authoritarian and harsh, but mostly it is desperate because at first he is not obeyed.
- The attempt to defy Papa is mirrored later (and earlier) in the novel when Jaja defies him on Palm Sunday.
- Kambili and Jaja watch this incident from a distance and by giving Kambili the words which describe the old man, Adichie suggests that the narrator feels some sympathy for him.
- Few people confront Papa in *Purple Hibiscus*. Ifeoma does it obliquely sometimes but she does not want to make things more difficult for her sister-in-law and her niece and nephew. Here this feisty old man openly reprimands Papa for lack of respect for his elders. He has the last word and leaves with his dignity intact, flanked by his friends, unlike Papa who has grown angrier and angrier.
- 'You are like a fly blindly following a corpse into the grave' is a colourful, and as it turns out accurate, description of Papa's mentality.

Jaja

Jaja says

- 'The wafer gives me bad breath.' (p. 6)
- 'I have nothing to say.' (p. 13)
- 'Papa-Nnukwu, we just ate before we came here [...]. If we're thirsty, we will drink in your house.' (p. 66)
- 'I wasted time. It was my fault.' (p. 69)
- 'I told her to eat corn flakes before she took Panadol, Papa. I made it for her.' (p. 102)
- 'Maybe he didn't want to convert.' (p. 191).
- 'The key to my room. I would like to have it. *Makana*, because I would like some privacy.' (p. 191)
- 'If Aunty Ifeoma leaves, then I want to leave with them, too.' (p. 235)
- 'I should have taken care of Mama. Look how Obiora balances Aunty Ifeoma's family on his head, and I am older than he is. I should have taken care of Mama.' (p. 289)

Pause for thought

Some readers and critics have said that Adichie does not develop the character of Jaja enough and that this slightly spoils the ending of the novel. What is your view?

Jaja

- is 17 years old
- is Kambili's elder brother
- is treated by Papa, as Kambili is, as a child to be controlled
- grows up physically and mentally through association with his cousins at Nsukka
- eventually finds courage to defy Papa on Palm Sunday
- tries, but usually fails, to protect his sister and mother at all times
- routinely deflects blame for things Kambili and Mama have done towards himself
- goes to prison for a murder he did not commit

Adichie presents Jaja

- as a young man gradually learning to think for himself
- as a contrast to Papa
- as a figure who often shares Kambili's experiences and memories
- as Kambili's only 'friend' until she gets to know her cousins better

Conclusions

Jaja is a troubled young man who knows that he ought, somehow, to be supporting his mother and sister but is not, at 17, strong enough to withstand his dictatorial, narrow-thinking father — until the Palm Sunday incident when he refuses to take communion. After that, he assertively tells his father that he and Kambili will return to Nsukka for Easter, making their own way there if Papa will not allow Kevin to drive them (p. 261).

Adichie shows us that Jaja has learned a great deal through watching family life in Ifeoma's house where the children are encouraged to think for themselves, laugh and grow up naturally. While there he has, presumably, made a quiet decision that when he gets home he will (must?) assert himself against Papa — who has, by this stage in the novel, caused his wife several miscarriages, deliberately mutilated one of Jaja's fingers, scalded his children's feet and nearly killed Kambili. It is in Ifeoma's house that Kambili notices signs of Jaja's physically becoming a man too (p. 154).

Jaja's first attempt at assertiveness fails. When he and Kambili return from the first visit to Nsukka, Jaja tells his father that he would like to keep his own bedroom key, but this leads to the foot scalding because 'being with a heathen has...taught them evil' (p. 192).

> **Key quotation**
>
> I followed Jaja out to the backyard, watched him hold the [chicken's] wings down under his foot. [...] There was a precision in Jaja, a singlemindedness that was cold, clinical.
>
> (Kambili, p. 235)

> **Key quotation**
>
> [His eyes] have hardened a little every month he has spent here; now they look like the bark of a palm tree, unyielding.
>
> (Kambili describing Jaja in prison, p. 305)

Eventually we see Jaja punishing himself for his failure to stop the abuse and doing what he believes he must do by confessing to the crime of poisoning Papa and going to prison, to save his mother.

Ifeoma

Ifeoma says

- 'Our father is dying, do you hear me? Dying. He is an old man, how much longer does he have, *gbo*? Yet Eugene will not let him into this house, will not even greet him. *O joka!* Eugene has to stop doing God's job.' (p. 95)
- 'Eugene, you must let the children come and visit us in Nsukka.' (p. 97)
- 'We do not say Mass in the name of grace like your father does.' (p. 119)
- 'Being defiant can be a good thing sometimes.' (p. 144)
- 'Kambili, have you no mouth? Talk back to her!' (p. 170)
- 'Has a nut come loose in your head, *gbo*? You are not going anywhere. [...] At least stay a few days, *nwunye m*, don't go back so soon.' (pp. 249–50)

Ifeoma

- is Papa's sister and aunt to Kambili and Jaja
- teaches at Nsukka University
- is widowed
- loved her husband
- has little money
- is bringing up her three children to be independent thinkers
- loves her elderly father and looks after him tenderly
- is a committed Catholic but respects traditional African religions
- disapproves of her brother's attitude and behaviour
- befriends Kambili and Jaja
- introduces Kambili to Father Amadi
- sympathises with her sister-in-law
- eventually takes her family to America for a better life

Adichie presents Ifeoma

- as a contrast to Papa to show that Catholicism does not have to be harsh, judgemental and joyless
- as a loving mother wanting to see her children develop and grow into thoughtful adults

- as the voice of common sense and decency, horrified, for example, by the injuries that Papa inflicts on Kambili (which put her in hospital for several weeks)
- as a contrast to Mama to show that women can be independent

Conclusions

Ifeoma has come from exactly the same background as Papa. She was born into a traditional, quite poor African family but educated in a mission school where she became a Catholic. But she is quite different from Papa in that she has not totally rejected her roots, looks after her elderly father with great tenderness (and encourages her children to do the same) and recognises that all religions are, at heart, quite similar. That is why she leads Kambili out to hear Papa-Nnukwu praying on the verandah (pp. 166–67). Adichie is presenting us with a woman of great intelligence, humanity and tolerance here.

Adichie uses Ifeoma to show that life is difficult under the military regime even for highly educated Nigerians, who do not happen — like Papa — to be successful industrialists. Ifeoma's husband, Ifediora, was killed in a road accident, so she is a single parent in a job where salaries are often not paid. She has little gas to cook with and has to cope with frequent power cuts and limited food supplies. She has to ask her brother for help with her father's funeral and the fares to America. Yet she is full of cheerfulness and laughter.

Nonetheless, she can also get angry. She is horrified by Kambili's hospitalisation and advises her sister-in-law to leave before anything worse happens, saying, 'This cannot go on, *nwunye m* […]. When a house is on fire, you run out before the roof collapses on your head' (p. 213). She also tries assertively to stop her sister-in-law taking the children back to Enugu (p. 250).

Ifeoma's migration to America at the end of the novel is part of Adichie's wider purpose in *Purple Hibiscus*: she typifies the many Nigerians who found that they could make a better life for themselves by leaving their native country than by staying in such an unstable place.

Mama

- is repeatedly injured by Papa, although rarely in front of the children
- loses two babies during the novel because of Papa's violence, and there have been earlier miscarriages
- was the daughter of an African Christian much admired by Papa (p. 67)

- polishes her china figurines whenever she has been hit by Papa
- talks to her children and tells them things which Papa does not
- is loyal to Papa
- often behaves lovingly towards Papa (p. 207)
- poisons Papa after the near-fatal attack on Kambili
- becomes deeply withdrawn after Papa's death and Jaja's imprisonment

> **Key quotation**
>
> '[...] sometimes
> life begins when
> marriage ends.'
>
> (Ifeoma, p. 75)

Papa-Nnukwu

- is Papa and Ifeoma's father
- is Kambili, Jaja, Amaka, Obiora and Chima's grandfather
- is visited in his basic Abba home by Kambili and Jaja at Christmas (pp. 63–67)
- goes on a day trip to Ezi Icheke with Ifeoma and all the grandchildren (pp. 82–87)
- worships traditional African gods and has a shrine in his yard
- is taken to Ifeoma's house to be cared for and dies there (p. 182)
- is rejected as a 'heathen' and 'idol worshipper' by Papa
- is used by Adichie to show the gentle humanity of the traditional Nigerian way of life
- is used by Adichie to show how a warm, loving, tolerant family operates

> **Key quotation**
>
> 'That young priest,
> singing in the
> sermon like a
> Godless leader of one
> of these Pentecostal
> churches that spring
> up everywhere
> like mushrooms.
> People like him
> bring trouble to the
> church.'
>
> (Papa about Father
> Amadi, p. 29)

Father Amadi

- is Ifeoma's Catholic priest at Nsukka
- is a close friend to Ifeoma and her family
- is young and attractive
- is the first black priest Kambili has ever known
- takes a warm and kindly interest in Kambili and Jaja
- is concerned about Kambili's unsmiling, repressed behaviour
- probably gets a little closer emotionally to Kambili than, as a Catholic priest, he should
- takes Kambili to the market to have her hair plaited (pp. 236–39)
- respects old traditions and weaves Igbo songs into his services
- helps provide sport for poor African boys
- goes with Ifeoma to visit Kambili in hospital
- is used by Adichie as a means of opening up Kambili's emotions
- is used by Adichie as a contrast to white priests such as Father Benedict

> **Key quotation**
>
> 'You can do anything
> you want, Kambili.'
>
> (Father Amadi to
> Kambili, p. 239)

He was looking right into my eyes.
He was too close. His touch was
so light I wanted to push my head
toward him, to feel the pressure of
his hand. I wanted to collapse against
him. I wanted to press his hand to my
head, my belly, so he could feel the
warmth that coursed through me.

(Kambili, p. 227)

Pause for thought

Kambili, 15 years old, is falling
in love with Father Amadi and
experiencing sexual longing
that she does not understand.
What do you think is going on
in the mind of 20-something
Father Amadi, a celibate
Catholic priest?

Pause for thought

Ifeoma's home is full of
books (p. 114) and there
are several references to
them. Although Kambili
and Jaja are made to
'study' for long periods
every day, we hear little
about books in their
home. What do you think
this tells us about the
differences between the
two households?

Amaka

- is Ifeoma's 15-year-old daughter
- is first cousin to Kambili
- has been brought up to think, reason and question
- lives in a family where money is short
- is initially jealous of Kambili's wealth
- later realises that Kambili is to be pitied
- adores Papa-Nnukwu
- is bright and talented
- has friends
- wears make-up and cheerful clothes
- is a champion of native traditions such as African music
- is often outspoken

TopFoto

Nigerian musician Fela
Kuti, Amaka's favourite
singer.

Key quotation

'It was Uncle Eugene who did that to you, *okwia?*' she asked.

I let go of the railings, suddenly needing to ease myself. Nobody had asked, not even the doctor at the hospital or Father Benedict. I did not know what Papa had told them. Or if he had even told them anything. 'Did Aunty Ifeoma tell you?' I asked.

'No, but I guessed so.'

(Amaka talking to Kambili, p. 220)

Other characters

Sisi. Indoor servant to Kambili's family, she is present throughout all the difficulties and well aware of what is going on. Her function in the novel is quietly to be Mama's main friend and support. Sisi provides Mama with the poison to kill Papa and continues caringly to call (p. 298) even after she has moved on.

Father Benedict. Cold, white priest at St Agnes, he rigidly hears Kambili's confessions. He turns a blind eye to Papa's violence at home because of Papa's 'good works' and cash donations at the church. He is one of the few white characters in the novel and a contrast to Father Amadi.

Obiora. Ifeoma's elder son, he tries to be the man of the house and, casually but unintentionally, models strong filial behaviour for Jaja. He is bright and can be rude (Ifeoma reprimands him for this, p. 245). When he reaches America, he wins a scholarship to a good school (p. 301).

Kevin. Trusted chauffeur who takes the children to school and elsewhere, he also does errands for Papa such as taking modest sums of money to Papa-Nnukwu (p. 67). He is supportive and genuinely caring towards Papa (p. 262). He has a dagger-shaped scar on his neck which Kambili finds sinister. After Papa's death, Mama dismisses Kevin (p. 295) and hires gentle-voiced Celestine.

Ade Coker. Editor of the *Standard*, owned by Papa, he writes outspoken anti-government articles, encouraged by Papa. He is killed by a letter bomb (p. 206), which devastates Papa and precedes Kambili's worst beating. Ade's function in the novel is to show how an educated Nigerian can have, unlike Papa, a relaxed family life and to remind the reader of the wider political situation in Nigeria.

Key quotation

'You understand that it is wrong to take joy in pagan rituals, because it breaks the first commandment. Pagan rituals are misinformed superstition, and they are the gateway to Hell.'

(Father Benedict, p. 106)

Key quotation

'They are always so quiet,' he said, turning to Papa. 'So quiet.'

(Ade Coker referring to Kambili and Jaja, p. 57)

(Answers on p. 92)

Review your learning

1. How does Ifeoma show what she thinks of her brother's attempt to control his children's time while they are staying with her?

2. What is unusual, in *Purple Hibiscus*, about Father Benedict and Sister Lucy?

3. What are the names of: a) Ifeoma's late husband, b) the family cook and maid, and c) Amaka and Obiora's younger brother?

4. Mama insists on returning to Enugu with the children against Ifeoma's advice (p. 250). What is her real reason?

5. What do Sisi and Kevin add to the symmetry of the novel?

6. Why does Mama simply not pack up and leave Papa?

More interactive questions and answers online.

Themes

- **What are the novel's main themes?**
- **What do they add to the novel?**
- **How do themes work?**

A theme is an idea, or a set of ideas, threaded through a piece of writing. Think of *Purple Hibiscus* as a piece of multi-coloured fabric. A theme is a single-coloured thread — red, blue, yellow and so on. Each thread is woven into the whole as part of the pattern. It mixes with the other colours that it crosses to make shapes or new colours. All the threads overlap. In the same way, Adichie weaves her ideas about religious differences, growing up and the long-term effects of colonialism into the story that she is telling.

When we discuss a theme, it is as if we are pulling out a single thread from the novel's overall pattern. We can look at it on its own and then weave it back into the whole.

The themes in *Purple Hibiscus* that will be considered here are:

- family
- tolerance
- conflict between Roman Catholic Christianity and traditional African religion
- dictatorship
- growing up
- education

Lesser, but related, themes include:

- relationships between grandchildren and grandparents
- marriage
- racism
- meals and food

Remember the following three points as you think about the themes in this novel:

1. No theme in a novel is completely separate from any other. They all overlap. That is what makes a text such as *Purple Hibiscus* feel complete.

2. Similar themes are often discussed using different names. For example, family conflict between Christianity and African religions is similar to religious intolerance, bigotry or cultural tension, and dictatorship is

close to tyranny, autocracy or absolute control. Do not get too carried away in compiling long, repetitive lists of themes.

3 Some themes feature more regularly than others in the pattern of the novel.

Family

The family at the heart of *Purple Hibiscus* consists of Papa, Mama, Kambili and Jaja. Adichie shows us their life together in more detail than any of the other families because Kambili, as narrator, has first-hand experience of her own family. Others in the novel she can describe only by observation or hearsay.

We learn how the members of Kambili's family relate to the dictatorial, bigoted, but loving and generous Papa as we are told about his repeated violence against his wife and harsh punishments for Kambili and Jaja if they stray, even in minor ways, from his interpretation of Roman Catholic rules. Mama, Kambili and Jaja often function in the novel as a silent trio trying to support Papa and yet suffering a great deal in many ways. All four are deeply unhappy. The atmosphere is tense and never relaxed; Kambili does not laugh or smile.

Adichie contrasts this with the freedom and laughter of Ifeoma's family and Kambili notices how her aunt encourages her children to be themselves in the same way as a football coach tries to develop his team (pp. 120–21). Although her husband died in an accident and they have little money, Ifeoma and her three children are a well-bonded family unit freely working together (p. 140) and cheerfully bantering at meal times (p. 120).

Ade Coker's is another example of a family in *Purple Hibiscus* that is different from Kambili's. When they call on Kambili's family at Abba, we see Ade cheerfully and joyfully playing with his baby by tossing him in the air (p. 57). Just before Ade is killed, his wife is spooning food into the baby's mouth as the child sits in a high chair at family breakfast — an image of happy domestic peace (p. 206) before the opening of the fatal package.

There are glimpses of other contrasting families in *Purple Hibiscus*. For example, when Papa-Nnukwu mentions allowing his son to attend

---

Key quotation

We always spoke with a purpose back home, especially at the table, but my cousins seemed to simply speak and speak and speak.

(Kambili, p. 120)

Key quotation

It was what Aunty Ifeoma did to my cousins, I realized then, setting higher and higher jumps for them in the way she talked to them, in what she expected of them. She did it all the time believing they would scale the rod. And they did. It was different for Jaja and me. We did not scale the rod because we believed we could, we scaled it because we were terrified that we couldn't.

(Kambili, p. 226)

Mission school, we get a reminder that he (and presumably his wife, who is never mentioned) once formed a traditional Nigerian family unit with Eugene and Ifeoma, although his son now refuses to see him because he will not convert to Christianity. Also, when Chinwe beats Kambili and comes first at school, she is taken to London by her father as a reward (p. 50) — a picture of a much warmer, gentler family than Kambili's.

Tolerance

The best example of tolerance in *Purple Hibiscus* is Ifeoma's respect for her father's traditional culture and religion. She is more than happy to visit him at his own home and to bring him to hers when he is ill and needs help. Wanting Kambili to see the beauty and humanity of the traditional prayers, Ifeoma wakes Kambili at dawn and takes her onto the verandah to see her grandfather at prayer (pp. 166–69). This attitude is a direct contrast with her brother's intolerance.

Father Amadi, quite unlike Father Benedict (p. 106), is warm and welcoming towards Papa-Nnukwu, clearly quite comfortable to show respect for the old man's age and religion' (p. 172). He even helps Ifeoma to bring him to Nsukka (p. 149). Adichie is using this to show that Christianity need not be dictatorial and intolerant (as it is for Papa).

Tolerance, of course, works in both directions. Just as Ifeoma and Father Amadi are tolerant of Papa-Nnukwu's ways (and Papa is intolerant of them), so Papa-Nnukwu cheerfully accepts that his daughter and son have different beliefs and attitudes from his.

> **Key quotation**
>
> 'I will put my dead husband's grave up for sale, Eugene, before I give our father a Catholic funeral. Do you hear me? I said I will sell Ifediora's grave first! Was our father a Catholic? I ask you, Eugene, was he a Catholic?'
>
> (Ifeoma, p. 189)

> **Key quotation**
>
> 'My brother, Eugene, almost single-handedly finances that church. Lovely church.' (Ifeoma, page 136)

> **Pause for thought**
>
> When Kambili watches Papa-Nnukwu praying, she notices that he smiles when he's finished. 'I never smiled after we said the rosary back home. None of us did', Adichie makes her say (p. 169). What does this tell you about Papa-Nnukwu's attitude to life compared with his son's?

Conflict between Christianity and traditional African religion

Not only does Adichie present religious conflict through the relationship between Papa, Ifeoma and Papa-Nnukwu, she also shows us how Kambili's late maternal grandfather embraced the 'new' religion with enthusiasm. Mama's father, who died when Kambili was ten, was light-skinned, welcomed the missionaries, learned English and Latin (for Catholic services) quickly and converted most of Abba (pp. 67–68). In doing this, Kambili's 'Grandfather' (as she was made to call him in English) was turning his back on all the traditional ways to which Papa-Nnukwu, in contrast, remained loyal.

We also see the conflict when Anikwenwa (pp. 69–70) arrives in Papa's compound. He is a contemporary of Papa-Nnukwu and, as such, has probably known Papa all his life. He thinks he is entitled to respect but he seems to know he will get none. There is no welcome for him. Papa refers to him angrily as 'a worshipper of idols' and has him evicted. Adichie uses this incident to show us the tensions between the 'old' and the 'new' ways of religion which are never far below the surface in *Purple Hibiscus*.

The theme is further developed in Ifeoma's taking the children to watch the traditional festival at Ezi Icheke (pp. 85–88), about which Papa has so many misgivings.

Notice, too, how frightened Papa is of being — or of his family's being — influenced by African religion and slipping back to it. He will not allow his children to have contact with traditionalists (only 15 minutes a year with their grandfather and no refreshments, for example) and he condemns 'speaking in tongues' (speaking incomprehensibly or in another language while in a religious trance), even though he does it himself when he gets particularly distraught (p. 208).

Key quotation

'One day I said to them, Where is this god you worship? They said he was like *Chukwu*, that he was in the sky. I asked then, Who is the person that was killed, the person that hangs on the wood outside the mission? They said he was the son, but that the son and the father are equal. It was then that I knew that the white man was mad. The father and the son are equal? *Tufia!* Do you not see? That is why Eugene can disregard me, because he thinks we are equal.'

(Papa-Nnukwu, p. 84)

Key quotation

Papa prayed for our protection from ungodly people and forces, for Nigeria and the Godless men ruling it, and for us to continue to grow in right-eousness. Finally, he prayed for the conversion of our Papa-Nnukwu, so that Papa-Nnukwu would be saved from hell.

(Kambili, p. 61)

Dictatorship

Papa is a dictator in his own home. He lays down precisely how the household is to be run. The children have no free time. Every minute of their waking day is formally scheduled. Most of this is done in the name of religion — a 20-minute grace of prayer session before each meal, for instance — but actually, as Kambili comments bleakly, 'Papa liked order' (p. 23).

He also likes to control as many people as possible outside his own household. He gives so much money to his church that he is treated as an important person there and it is one of the reasons Father Benedict does not interfere with the way Papa manages his family. At Abba he is an 'omelora' (pp. 55–56), the equivalent of the local lord of the manor, with hundreds of people partly dependent on him. He also controls his factories and his newspaper the *Standard*, which Ade Coker edits.

When his absolute control of his life is damaged first by Ade Coker's death — and the consequent guilt, regret and anger — and then by Jaja's rebellion on Palm Sunday, Papa begins to lose his strength. It is after Ade Coker's murder that he injures Kambili so badly. When Jaja begins to assert himself, Papa realises his power is gone. It is, in effect, a family coup.

Meanwhile, Adichie develops the dictatorship theme beyond the main characters, too. Big Oga — an Igbo term for 'Big Boss' and a status many Nigerian men aspire to — is what Ade Coker calls the military dictator who sends letter bombs to journalists who write stories he would rather they did not and who sends raiders to frighten Ifeoma (pp. 230–31). Papa claims to loathe all this and argues for 'renewed democracy' (p. 25), but Adichie makes it clear that there is no democracy — only dictatorship — in his own life and invites us to compare his household with Ifeoma's enlightened, free-thinking one.

A Nigerian street market.

Text **focus**

Read from 'Mama Joe's shed in Ogige market...' on p. 236 to the end of the section on p. 239.

Notice how Adichie describes this African market with its 'wheelbarrows and pigs and people and chickens' and conveys its remoteness from Kambili's luxurious home.

She achieves the ramshackle sense of the market where people are scratching a basic living (Mama Joe relies on Ifeoma's cast-off clothes and Ifeoma herself is poor by Kambili's standards) by using breathless lists of what Kambili observes, such as 'twisting hair, weaving hair, plaiting hair with thread'.

Mama Joe, kindly, cheerful and chatty as she is, seems faintly repellent to Kambili. Mama Joe is dirty. She spits on her hands and her blouse is stained with sweat. Barefooted, she stamps on a cockroach. Kambili, in contrast, comes from a home where everyone washes frequently, almost ritualistically. Mama Joe notices Father Amadi's tenderness with Kambili and teases her about it just as Amaka does back at Ifeoma's flat. Twice her garrulousness leaves Kambili not knowing what to say. Adichie is reminding us that Kambili finds casual conversation difficult because all communication is formal in her home. The snails — gathered for sale by children — are alive and trying to escape from the basket. One in particular seems 'enterprising' and 'determined' and Kambili sympathises with the maverick one, imagining the snails' fate as 'fried to a crisp, warped corpses floating' in the soup pot of the woman who eventually buys them.

This incident is part of Kambili's growing up. She has been brought here to a traditional hairdresser by a 'broad shouldered' man she fantasises about. Before this, her hair has always been put into cornrows, childlike, by her mother.

Notice the carefully chosen adjectives that Adichie uses in this passage, which bring the market and Kambili's experience there to life: 'lopsided', 'brown', 'spiralled', 'squeaky', 'smooth', 'melodious'. Also note how Adichie's verbs make her writing succinct and accurate without being obscure or difficult: 'welcomed', 'retrieved', 'protested'. The author gives Kambili, looking back as an adult, a very natural voice.

Grade *focus*

When you are writing about the theme of the family, the examiners will want to see that you understand how Adichie approaches it from several directions and at different levels. Use the table below to give yourself a clearer idea of the difference between a higher- and foundation-tier answer to a question about family in *Purple Hibiscus*.

Grades A*–C points	Grades D–G points
Adichie presents Kambili's immediate family in detail and invites us to compare other families such as Ifeoma's and Ade Coker's with it.	There are a lot of families in *Purple Hibiscus*.
Every member of Kambili's family is, in his or her own way — even Papa — deeply unhappy and disturbed. Mama and Jaja both worry about protecting each other and Kambili, while Papa is constantly worrying about the perceived misdemeanours of his family and devastated with guilt and grief after the death of Ade Coker.	Kambili and Jaja do not live in a happy family.
Adichie uses the different attitudes of Ifeoma and Papa to their elderly, dying father to show another sort of family relationship. She develops this by presenting Ifeoma's children as loving grandchildren from whom Kambili and Jaja learn that their father's way is not necessarily right.	Papa won't see his old father or have him in the house. The old man dies in Ifeoma's flat.

Growing up

Kambili herself grows up and changes during the course of the novel, especially during the year which precedes Palm Sunday and after Papa's death when she suddenly has to change from being a repressed 15-year-old child to a woman who can support her mother and make important decisions while Jaja is in prison. The main influences which change her are getting to know Ifeoma and her family better, spending time with Papa-Nnukwu at the end of his life and, of course, her father's death, brother's imprisonment and mother's near breakdown.

At the same time, Adichie shows us Kambili noticing how Jaja is changing and growing up too. He seems to mature physically while they are at Ifeoma's and quite quickly learns from his cousins how to express a view and speak up for himself. It is this experience that gives him the courage first to ask for the key to his room and then to refuse to take communion on Palm Sunday when things 'started to fall apart at home'.

Amaka, Obiora and Chima have to grow up too, although Chima is young and Adichie does not develop him much. Amaka learns as much from Kambili as Kambili does from her, eventually soberly realising what Kambili has been through to put her in hospital. Amaka does not want to leave Nigeria, her friends and her music and go to America (p. 232) but has to find the maturity to accept that it is for the best (p. 301), although she reports that in the USA they are all too busy to laugh any more.

> **Key quotation**
>
> I looked away. Amaka took my hand in hers. It felt warm, like the hand of someone just recovering from malaria. She did not speak, but I felt as though we were thinking the same thing—how different it was for Jaja and me.
>
> (Kambili, p. 246)

> **Key quotation**
>
> I laughed. It seemed so easy now, laughter. So many things seemed easy now. Jaja was laughing, too, as was Amaka [...].
>
> (Kambili, p. 284)

> **Pause for thought**
>
> It's easy to think of children and teenagers growing up but do you think any of the adults in *Purple Hibiscus* grow up — perhaps maturing, changing or developing — too?

Education

In one sense the theme of education in *Purple Hibiscus* is wide because it could be extended to include every character's learning about everything. Here, though, only Adichie's presentation of formal education will be considered.

Kambili and Jaja both attend single-sex, fee-charging Catholic schools to and from which they are driven daily by Kevin (p. 22) or occasionally Papa (p. 44). Their teachers are white and they are taught exactly the same sort of curriculum as in a British school. For instance, Kambili mentions her *'Introductory Technology* textbook' (p. 22). They have assignments — homework — to do in the evening and at weekends and Papa specifies blocks of study time even during school holidays (p. 24). Papa expects Kambili to come first in everything, even sports (p. 51). Kambili's teachers are quite kind and encouraging (pp. 38–39) and Adichie implicitly compares their attitude to learning with Papa's unreasonable one (p. 39).

Meanwhile Amaka, Obiora and Chima attend schools on the university complex where their mother works. Like everything else at the university, the schools are in difficulties. At Chima's primary school, the building is being allowed to delapidate (p. 129). They are different from the schools Kambili and Jaja attend in Enugu. Nevertheless Ifeoma's children are clearly encouraged, to some extent, by their school teachers to think and reason for themselves — just as they are at home.

When Ifeoma's family arrives in America, Obiora wins a scholarship to a private school where 'he is praised and not punished for challenging his teachers' (p. 301). Adichie is making it clear to the reader that Obiora's education will, in the future, ensure that he prospers in the USA.

As a university lecturer, long denied the promotion she deserves, Ifeoma is a professional educator, which shows in her encouraging attitude to her own children. Adichie presents her as a bookish, but practical, woman who cares about her own students, such as the one who calls (pp. 233–34) to say that she is giving up college to get married. Ifeoma is quietly sympathetic to the students who riot (p. 228) because they are dissatisfied with the education provided under the university's 'sole administrator' — another dictator. She does not, however, incite the riot, although she is accused of it (p. 231) and eventually loses her job (p. 261).

There are also children on the edges of *Purple Hibiscus* who, in contrast to Kambili, her brother and cousins, are getting no

---

> ### Key quotation
>
> 'I didn't have a father who sent me to the best schools. My father spent his time worshiping gods of wood and stone. I would be nothing today but for the priests and sisters at the mission. [...] Nobody dropped me off at school. I walked eight miles every day to Nimo until I finished elementary school. I was a gardener for the priests while I attended St. Gregory's Secondary School.'
>
> (Papa, p. 47).

> ### Key quotation
>
> The walls that surrounded Daughters of the Immaculate Heart Secondary School were very high, similar to our compound walls, but instead of coiled electrified wires, they were topped by jagged pieces of green glass with sharp edges jutting out. Papa said the walls had swayed his decision when I finished elementary school. Discipline was important, he said. You could not have youngsters scaling walls to go into town and go wild, the way they did at the federal government colleges.'
>
> (Kambili, p. 45)

> ### Key quotation
>
> 'The university is living on past glory nowadays.'
>
> (Papa, page 97)

> ### Pause for thought
>
> Do you think Adichie is obliquely suggesting that Papa has reasons for selecting Daughters of the Immaculate Heart Secondary School for Kambili other than the ones he tells her about?

formal education at all: Mama Joe's nieces and nephews who gather the lakeside snails for sale at the market (p. 239), for example, or the 'hawkers, girls much younger than I' selling fruit near Kambili's school (p. 45).

Review your learning

(Answers on p. 92)

1. How old was Kambili when her maternal grandfather died?
2. What is Ade Coker's wife doing when the letter bomb reaches her husband?
3. Who is Big Oga?
4. Why does Adichie mention the children outside Kambili's school (p. 45)?
5. What, for Adichie, is the key difference between the way Kambili and Jaja are being brought up and the way their cousins are being brought up?
6. If you had to choose just one, which would you say is the novel's strongest theme? Give reasons for your answer.

More interactive questions and answers online.

Style

- How does the author tell her story?
- From whose point of view does the reader learn about events and characters?
- When and where is the novel set and what effect does this have?
- How much use does Adichie make of symbolism?
- What use does Adichie make of colourful description?
- What sort of language does she use and why?

Viewpoint

The story is told entirely by Kambili Achike. As she is part of the events and situations she is describing, she uses personal pronouns such as 'I', 'me', 'mine', 'we', 'us' and 'ours'. This technique is known as first-person narrative. Many famous books have been written in this format, including *Great Expectations* by Charles Dickens (1861), *Jane Eyre* by Charlotte Brontë (1848), *To Kill a Mockingbird* by Harper Lee (1960) and *The Curious Incident of the Dog in the Night-Time* by Mark Haddon (2003).

Text focus

Look at the passage on pp. 112–13, from 'Marguerite Cartwright Avenue was bordered...' to '...stamping down hard.' Read it carefully several times.

- The first part of the passage is descriptive writing in which Adichie makes Kambili's narrative move in, like a film, towards Ifeoma's home as the car gets closer to it.
- Kambili has not seen the university or Ifeoma's home before. Adichie is giving the reader Kambili's first impressions.
- In places, Kambili's observations are imaginative ('I imagined the trees bending during a rainy-season thunderstorm, reaching across to touch each other and turning the avenue into a dark tunnel'), and elsewhere they are stark and factual ('Aunty Ifeoma's was on the ground floor on the left').
- Marguerite Cartwright Avenue becomes increasingly less luxurious as the car passes first spacious apartments ('duplexes'), then smaller bungalows and finally shabby blocks of flats.
- Implicit in this description is the contrast between the flat Ifeoma's family live in and Kambili's luxurious homes at Enugu and Abba. That is why Adichie has her notice details such as 'peeling blue paint' and 'barbed wire'.

- Ifeoma's 'circular burst of bright colors' in front of her flat makes it stand out and is, in a sense, symbolic of the happy family she heads. There is nothing as relaxed and pretty as 'a hand-painted wreath' where Kambili comes from.
- When Ifeoma comes out to greet her guests, everything about her is informal, natural and friendly — her casual clothing, her speech and manner.
- Her reaction of delight — literally dancing for joy — when she realises her brother/sister-in-law has sent her gas cylinders is uninhibited and unself-conscious. She is presented here as quite different from the other adults in Kambili's life.
- Adichie shows us, via Kambili's narrative, that Kevin is uneasy about this assignment — he drives slowly and mutters the house number. But even he smiles when he meets Ifeoma. Adichie is giving us a subtle indication of her infectious cheerfulness and good humour.

Although first-person narratives are realistic, writing in this style presents the author with technical problems that would not exist if the story were told in the third person, i.e. by someone outside the story describing the activities, thoughts and views of the characters. Third-person narratives use pronouns such as 'he', 'she', 'his', 'her', 'they' and 'theirs'. J. K. Rowling's *Harry Potter* books and Michelle Magorian's *Goodnight Mister Tom* (1981) are examples of third-person narratives.

So, in a first-person narrative such as *Purple Hibiscus*, on the whole we hear only about things Kambili has seen and done and about the people she knows. Adichie has two main strategies for extending this.

The first is that other characters such as Mama, Papa, Jaja, Ifeoma and Ifeoma's children tell Kambili about things which Kambili has not witnessed. For example, Papa tells her, not for the first time, about his own education (p. 47). Amaka and Obiora tell Kambili about the misman-agement of the university and the difficulties it makes for their mother as an employee (pp. 223–24). It is Mama who tells Kambili what she and Papa have been told about Ade Coker (p. 207). We also learn a little of what Jaja has told Kambili about life in prison (p. 299). Adichie also has Kambili learn about things she has not personally experienced through other media such as the radio (p. 24) and letters (pp. 302–03).

Adichie's second technique for extending the narrative scope beyond Kambili's immediate experience is to have her overhear things which are not meant for her — a strategy used by most writers of first-person narratives, although Adichie does this less than some other authors. Examples in *Purple Hibiscus* include Kambili's hearing her father hitting her mother in their bedroom (pp. 32–33) and the passage where Kambili overhears Amaka asking Ifeoma whether Kambili and Jaja are 'abnormal' (pp. 141–42).

Text focus

Look at the passage on pp. 295–96, from 'The roads to the prison…' to '…not cutting her hair.' Read it carefully several times.

- After the drama and intensity of Kambili's last stay in Nsukka and Papa's death, this is a subdued passage. The contrast is part of the rhythm of Kambili's narrative and the way in which Adichie has structured the novel.
- Adichie has Kambili use the present tense to reinforce the immediacy of what is happening. It also works with the repetitiveness ('I know…', 'Perhaps…'), to make it clear to the reader that this is a journey which Kambili and Mama have made, separately, many times and occasionally together, as now.
- The other purpose of the present tense is to suggest that the novel is being 'told' now as Jaja is about to be released from prison. Everything else in the novel is Kambili looking back and recalling the past.
- We see that it is now Kambili who is in charge and making decisions because her mother is evidently suffering from the indecisiveness and apathy of a depressive. It is to Kambili that Celestine, the chauffeur, turns for instructions.
- Through Kambili's comments, Adichie wants us to compare Celestine, whose 'voice is gentle', with the dismissed Kevin who had a 'dagger-shape scar on his neck'. Kevin was closely attached to, and supportive of Papa. Mama has hired Celestine because, it is implied, she does not want to employ anyone associated with her dead husband.
- Mama, we see, has lost interest in her personal appearance. She neither knows nor cares how she looks. Her scarf is loose, her wrapper (which she keeps fiddling with) hangs untidily on her 'painfully bony body' and she has skin problems. These are clear signs of a depressive illness.
- Mama has not observed mourning conventions such as wearing all black or all white for a year and cutting her hair short. Neither did she attend the memorial masses said for Papa a year and two years after his death. People she knows — at church and elsewhere — wrongly assume (Kambili supposes) that this is all because she is lost in grief.
- In fact, Mama is ill because no one would believe her when she told the truth about Papa's death and she has to bear the guilt of Jaja's being in prison. 'She has been different ever since Jaja was locked up.'
- The style Adichie gives the 18-year-old Kambili here is different from the way she thinks and speaks earlier. Many of her sentences are short and terse from 'The roads to the prison are familiar' (p. 295) to '…they still don't' (p. 296). She is explaining the situation in a calm, colourless monotone. We are given the impression that the last two and a half years since Jaja's arrest at the end of the previous section have been difficult and have changed her as well as her mother.

Remember that there are two presentations of Kambili in *Purple Hibiscus*. First there is the teenaged girl, aged 15 and younger in the early 1990s, with a short section set three years later when she is 18. Then there is the adult Kambili, perhaps in her mid- to late 20s, looking back ten or so years later and describing her memories.

The first says subservient things such as 'God will deliver us' (p. 26), 'Good afternoon, Mama' (p. 39) and 'Yes, Papa' (three times, during the feet-scalding incident, p. 194). Gradually she learns to be a little less self-effacing and slightly more assertive through association with Ifeoma and her children. For example, she clumsily questions Father Amadi about his vocation (p. 179) and she asks Amaka what her mother has been discussing with her friend (p. 223), knowing that she 'would not have asked before'.

After Papa's death, when Kambili has to take charge of her mother, family finances and the household because everything has come 'tumbling down', her voice is more confident and adult. For instance, she says firmly, 'Mama, Jaja doesn't need knives' (p. 304) and 'You'll be out of here next week' (p. 305), although she is still brooding inside about Father Amadi and carrying his letters around because 'they remind me of my worthiness, because they tug at my feelings' (p. 303).

The second Kambili is the invisible narrator who is able to see a pattern in the events of her late childhood, with Palm Sunday and everything that led up to it and followed it as a major turning point.

> ### Key quotation
>
> **I laughed. It sounded strange, as if I were listening to the recorded laughter of a stranger being played back. I was not sure I had ever heard myself laugh.**
>
> (Kambili, p. 179)

Grade *focus*

How does Adichie use Kambili as a narrator?

Grades A*–C points	Grades D–G points
Adichie gives us, in Kambili, a narrator who describes what happens to her both as she experienced it in her teens and as an adult looking back thoughtfully.	The story is told from Kambili's point of view so she uses 'I'.
Beyond Kambili's immediate experience in the novel's present, Adichie presents her narrator's memories of things that happened when she was younger, such as the occasion when Father Amadi came to St Agnes (pp. 28 and 136) and the account of how Papa used to punish the younger Jaja and Kambili with sticks from the garden (p. 193).	Kambili looks back on things she can remember.
Kambili is told things by adults in her life which enables Adichie to build a vivid picture of what is going on in Nigeria beyond Kambili's home.	Grown-ups tell Kambili things.
Adichie occasionally contrives situations in which Kambili overhears others talking as a way of adding more depth to her narrative. She is present, but silent, for example, when Ifeoma and Mama discuss Papa's violence (pp. 248–49).	Kambili listens in on other people's conversations.

Pause for thought

Could Adichie have written *Purple Hibiscus* as a third-person narrative? What would have been gained and what would have been lost if she had chosen this format instead of the first person? Think about, for example:

- Kambili's frightened, half-understanding, observation of her father's personality. Would it have been as powerful if Kambili had been 'she' rather than 'I'?
- The account of Papa's childhood which we get from what he tells Kambili and what she learns from Ifeoma and Papa-Nnukwu. Might it have been better if the story had been told straightforwardly and the background filled in by an invisible narrator?

Setting and atmosphere

Purple Hibiscus is set entirely in Nigeria. The action moves from Enugu, where Kambili's main home is, south to Abba, Papa's ancestral home and where he maintains a large and impressive house (p. 55), and north to Nsukka where Ifeoma lives and works at the university. These places are quite near each other – all are in the south of the country, east of the river Niger and just north of its delta. It takes Ifeoma less than half a day (once she has petrol) to collect Papa-Nnukwu from Abba and drive him back to Nsukka (p. 151).

Text focus

Look at the passage on pp. 241–42, from 'There was no power...' to '...might have been miles away'. Read it carefully several times.

- This is highly atmospheric writing in which Adichie has Kambili describing what she sees and hears during a power cut at Nsukka.
- Her vibrant images ('blue-black blanket', lights like 'the eyes of hundreds of wild cats' and the description of the insects) help to convey an atmosphere of darkness and tension in which everyone is waiting for something to happen.
- The verandah is lit only by the 'gold-yellow lights of kerosene lamps' which focus Kambili's attention on the tiny movements of the insects drawn to the light, whose movements she observes closely.
- Adichie has Kambili use several short sentences here which add concision to her thoughts and reactions: 'She made to take one kerosene lamp', 'The dim light blurred her features', 'Her friend was silent a long time after Aunty Ifeoma finished her story.'
- Although there is tension here — as Ifeoma works towards her decision to leave Nigeria — this is also a peaceful scene depicting a secure family in which Amaka brings Father Amadi's greetings and Ifeoma gives practical instructions for keeping the insects out of the house.
- Ifeoma describes (without the detail or direct speech here because the reader already knows about it from Kambili's account on pp. 230–31) to her friend how her home was raided by security men. The friend's silent reaction and the apparent comments of the 'loud shrilling' crickets anticipate, or perhaps endorse, Ifeoma's final decision to take her three children to America.
- 'Dramatic urgency' refers not just to Ifeoma's story but also to the situation in which she now finds herself at the university.
- The calm manner (her smiles and her silence) and the physical appearance of Ifeoma's unnamed friend (the way she wore her 'bright tie-dye boubou and her short hair natural') indicate confidence and are part of Adichie's characterisation of this minor character who is an understanding support to Ifeoma in a way that her brother is not.
- This is a good example of the stress caused to ordinary people by the political situation in Nigeria and how they have to adapt.
- The Nigerian setting and atmosphere is enhanced by Adichie's description of the plants such as the hibiscuses, red and purple. Occasionally she mentions wildlife too, such as the *aku*, insects which fly at certain times of year, traditionally gathered by children and presented at home for cooking with *anara* leaves and red peppers (pp. 218–21).

The tropical seasons — the heavy rain through sunshine for example (p. 217) — or the dry, dusty harmattan wind which blows mainly from November to March add to the sense that Nigeria is climatically, and therefore atmospherically, different from, for example, Britain.

Adichie also carefully shows us what characters are eating as a way of evoking the Nigerian setting. European as the furniture and fittings in their houses are, Kambili's family eat in the traditional Nigerian way, using *fufu* (a cross between bread and a dumpling made from yams) as a staple just as Papa-Nnukwu and Ifeoma do. Amaka, however, is amused to see Kambili struggling to eat African food such as rice with a knife and fork, European-style (p. 97).

> **Key quotation**
>
> **Our yard was wide enough to hold a hundred people dancing atilogu, spacious enough for each dancer to do the usual somersaults and land on the next dancer's shoulders. The compound walls, topped by coiled electric wires, were so high I could not see the cars driving by on our street.**
>
> (Kambili, p. 9)

> **Key quotation**
>
> **It was early rainy season, and the frangipani trees planted next to the walls already filled the yard with the sickly-sweet scent of their flowers. A row of purple bougainvillea, cut smooth and straight as a buffet table, separated the gnarled trees from the driveway.**
>
> (Kambili, p. 9)

Lonely Planet Images/Alamy

A bowl of fufu, usually made from yams or cassava.

> **Pause for thought**
>
> What use does Adichie make of food in *Purple Hibiscus*? Make a list of meals described, with page references. Consider each food or meal, asking yourself why it is included and what it adds to the novel. Your notes could be a useful part of your revision.

> **Key quotation**
>
> **...as if she could not believe that anybody had to be told how to peel yam slices properly. She picked up the knife and started to peel a slice, letting only the brown skin go. I watched the measured movement of her hand and the increasing length of the peel, wishing I could apologize, wishing I knew how to do it right. She did it so well that the peel did not break, a continuous twirling soil-studded ribbon.**
>
> (Kambili describing Amaka, p. 134)

Kambili grows up in a restricted atmosphere. She has not travelled abroad as some girls at her school have (pp. 49–50). She leaves the family compound in Enugu only when driven by Papa or Kevin. Even when she goes with Mama to the market to buy school clothes, they are chauffeured by Kevin (p. 43).

At Abba, Papa allows them to make the short journey to Papa-Nnukwu's house only by car with Kevin. This is partly because of Papa's determination to control everything his children do, but it is also partly because Nigeria's political unrest could mean that the streets are unsafe. In the market at Enugu, for instance, Kambili sees vegetable stalls ruthlessly destroyed by soldiers (p. 44). Kevin, when Papa is not there, pays roadblock police bribes (p. 111). Kambili sees a man having his car searched by armed guards (p. 27) and later on there is an incident in which someone has been killed in an accident at a checkpoint (p. 103).

The atmosphere at Papa and Mama's is one of austerity, restriction and control. Both Papa's houses are compounds to which entrance is strictly controlled by his staff. Even in Abba at Christmas when the people that Papa regards as 'his' (his 'ummuna') come to meet ('greet') the family and cook celebratory food, the 'heathen' old man that Papa disapproves of is evicted (pp. 69–70). Within his houses, especially at Enugu during term time, there is a strict routine of prayer and study for the children, which leaves them no free time.

The atmosphere in Nsukka is quite different and Adichie is inviting us to make comparisons. Ifeoma's flat has only three rooms, plus the kitchen and a basic bathroom. Her children come and go independently — often calling on, or playing with, the children in other flats or going to the shop. They, too, pray (pp. 119 and 125) and study, and there are many books in the flat. Both Amaka and Obiora are well informed and articulate, but they also have free time during which they watch television (p. 125), and Amaka enjoys the music of indigenous African groups (p. 118) and chats to friends (p. 141).

Gradually, as Kambili and Jaja absorb the Nsukka atmosphere, it leads Jaja to question, and eventually challenge, the way of life in his own home.

Symbolism

The figurines on the étagère

Adichie uses Mama's fragile ornaments as a symbol of her struggles to cope with the way Papa treats her. Whenever Mama is physically hurt, she cleans and rearranges the ballet-dancing figurines. Once she knows that

Grade *booster*

To get the highest grades, refer to and comment on Adichie's presentation of the setting and how she uses it. Try to get beyond simply describing what the setting is — offer interpretations of what the effects are on the characters and on the reader.

Pause for thought

'A line of tiny ginger-colored ants marched near it.' Why do you think Adichie includes details such as this? What effect would it have had on the novel if she had left them out?

Papa is going to die, she no longer needs them, as Kambili recognises with hindsight years later (p. 15). Adichie weaves this symbol through the novel, making Kambili mention the figurines quite often as a signal to alert the reader to more marital abuse:

- Kambili recalls wondering 'years ago' why Mama polished the ornaments each time 'I heard the sounds from their room, like something being banged against the door' (p. 10).
- After the first miscarriage induced by Papa's blows, Mama works on the figurines, using water brought silently by Sisi who understands exactly what is going on (p. 35).
- Sisi and Mama's polishing of the figurines symbolises Papa having struck his wife. They both know that the polishing reflects the violence but neither mentions it aloud (see for example p. 35).
- Two weeks before Palm Sunday, Mama has both cleaned and rearranged the ornaments 'when her swollen eye was still the black-purple color of an overripe avocado' (pp. 10–11).
- The ornaments are smashed on Palm Sunday by Papa throwing his prayer book, symbolising the beginning of the end of life as Kambili has always known it (pp. 3, 7, 253 and 257–58).

Pause for thought

Go through *Purple Hibiscus* and make notes on each occasion Mama talks about Papa and her marriage. Can you work out why she keeps the marriage going as long as she does? This is not a simple matter. There is, almost certainly, more than one reason.

Key quotation

'You know that small table where we keep the family Bible, *nne*? Your father broke it on my belly.' She sounded as if she were talking about someone else, as if the table were not made of sturdy wood. 'My blood finished on the floor even before he took me to St. Agnes. My doctor said there was nothing he could do to save it.'

(Mama to Kambili and Ifeoma, telling the truth openly for the first time, p. 248)

Key quotation

I could not even think of her and Papa together, on the bed they shared, custom-made and wider than the conventional king-size. When I thought of affection between them, I thought of them exchanging the sign of peace at Mass, the way Papa would hold her tenderly in his arms after they had clasped hands.

(Kambili, p. 25)

Purple hibiscus

As we have seen in the *Context* section of this guide, most hibiscuses are red and the purple ones that the children first see growing in Ifeoma's garden are unusual. Adichie uses the purple hibiscus, developed by a friend of Ifeoma's in the university botany department (Phillipa), as a symbol of hope for a free future. It is threaded through her novel as well as providing its title. See, for example, these references:

- Jaja first notices and comments on the purple hibiscus (p. 128). We are reminded that life at Ifeoma's is different from that at the children's family home.

Jaja's defiance seemed to me now like Aunty
Ifeoma's experimental purple hibiscus: rare, fragrant
with the undertones of freedom, a different kind
of freedom from the one the crowds waving green
leaves chanted at Government Square after the coup.
A freedom to be, to do.

(Kambili, p. 16)

Key quotation

Jaja's eyes shone as he talked about
the hibiscuses, as he held them out so
I could touch the cold, moist sticks.
He had told Papa about them, yet he
quickly put them back into the fridge
when we heard Papa coming.

(Kambili, p. 197)

Grade *booster*

For a high grade,
make it clear in an
exam essay about
how Adichie uses
the purple hibiscus
motif in her novel that
you are aware that a
symbol is something
small and tangible or
ordinary which stands
for something large and
intangible (for example,
a nation's flag stands
for its land, culture and
values). Here the purple
hibiscus symbolises
Jaja and Kambili's
freedom.

- Kambili comments that before Palm Sunday their hibiscuses were still 'a startling red' (p. 16) because nothing had yet changed in Papa's household.
- Jaja tells Ifeoma that the stalks she gave him are planted at Enugu but 'it was still too early to tell if they would live' (p. 202). Adichie wants us to apply that comment to the way of thinking that Jaja has brought back from Nsukka along with the plant cuttings.
- 'See, the purple hibiscuses are about to bloom' says Jaja the day before he defies his father on Palm Sunday (p. 253).
- Kambili plans that when Jaja is released from prison he will plant purple hibiscus — a symbol of freedom (pp. 306–07).

Imagery

Using imagery means describing one thing by comparing it with pictures — images — of other things that are in some way similar. It is closely related to imagination, a word that comes from the same root in Latin. Imagery is an 'umbrella term' that includes similes, metaphors and personification. Sometimes the term 'figurative language' is used instead of imagery.

Key quotation

...like a rooster in charge of all the
neighborhood hens.

(Kambili using a simile to describe Father
Amadi at the football stadium, p. 178)

Key quotation

He bounded up the few stairs to the
verandah, holding his soutane up like a
bride holding a wedding dress.

(Kambili using a simile to describe Father
Amadi arriving at Ifeoma's flat, p. 171)

When Kambili describes her father's face 'breaking open like a coconut with the brilliant white meat inside' when he smiles (p. 25), or the dislodged satellite dish that 'lounged on the driveway like a visiting alien spaceship' (p. 257), or the sun that 'came out again, mildly, as if yawning after a nap' (p. 266), Adichie is using similes.

A simile is a comparison which uses 'like' or 'as' to make it clear that two things are being likened to each other. Similes are part of the voice that Adichie creates for Kambili and they are often part of the Nigerian setting because she usually colours her observations by comparing people and actions with what is around them. For example, she compares the insects with a 'black string, a mobile necklace' (p. 218) and the blows from her father's slippers' metal buckles when he kicks her with 'bites from giant mosquitoes' (p. 210). These are African images.

By contrast, a metaphor makes the comparison without using 'like' or 'as'. Instead it pretends that the thing or action being described actually is the image created. For example, when Kambili recalls Obiora's fascination with the stereo player's 'chrome entrails' (p. 93), she is using a metaphor. It is a slightly humorous way of referring to the inner workings of an inanimate machine. Kambili also uses a metaphor when she remembers Nsukka as a place where 'the air smells of hills and history and sunlight scatters the sand and turns it into gold dust' (p. 299). This is a metaphorical — and rather poetic and romantic — way of describing her feelings for Nsukka. In literal terms, there is no 'smell of history' and no 'gold dust'. Another example is 'the leather sofas' greeting' which 'was a clammy coldness' (p. 192). However, in general, Adichie uses many more similes than metaphors.

Kambili also describes things using personification, conveying the properties of something inanimate (without life of its own) by pretending that it has human qualities or those of a person, hence the term personification. For instance, she observes that 'the harmattan wind tore across the front yard', as if it were a person in a hurry (p. 189). Adichie also has Kambili give abstract nouns, such as laughter and dawn, the strong animate verbs 'floated' (p. 71) and 'trickled' (p. 167) — another form of personification.

Imagery is sometimes linked to symbolism. In *Purple Hibiscus*, meals are one example. The solemn meals that Kambili sits down to with her parents and brother, and the image of them, are part of the laughter-free ritual of her home life. They are contrasted with the relaxed, chatty mealtimes (with much less food) at Ifeoma's. Mealtimes are referred to so much that they come to stand for African family life and solidarity, in all its different forms (Ade Coker was killed during a family meal too). They become a symbol.

Language

Purple Hibiscus is written in English because in Nigeria English is the official language of government and education — a result of its colonial past. English is the language in which Chimamanda Ngozi Adichie was taught at her elementary and secondary schools in Nigeria in the 1980s and 1990s. 'The way we are is very much the result of our colonialism — the fact that I think in English, for example,' she has said.

Key quotation

The silence he left was heavy but comfortable, like a well-worn, prickly cardigan on a bitter morning.

(Kambili using a simile to describe a moment after Papa has left the room, p. 69)

Pause for thought

Why do you think Adichie repeatedly mentions Ifeoma's 'cackling, hearty' laughter? (p. 71)

Grade *booster*

You will get few marks for spotting and identifying an example of imagery. The highest-scoring essays comment on the effects of similes and metaphors rather than just noticing that the author uses them.

Grade *booster*

To show that you understand that *Purple Hibiscus* uses American spellings and some grammar conventions, use exactly the language that Adichie uses in quotations, enclosed in quotation marks. Do not 'correct' her spelling. (Apart from in quotations, however, use British English conventions in your exam answers.)

Key quotation

...sometimes I understood him a moment or two after he spoke because his dialect was ancient; his speech had none of the anglicized inflections that ours had.

(Kambili describing Papa Nnukwu, p. 64)

Key quotation

I was in my room after lunch, reading James chapter five because I would talk about the biblical roots of the anointing of the sick during family time, when I heard the sounds.

(Kambili, p. 32)

In *Purple Hibiscus*, Adichie uses the American form of English because she attended universities in the USA and the novel was first published there. This is why, for instance Ifeoma's children call her 'Mom' rather than 'Mum', why the place they buy soft drinks is a 'store' rather than a 'shop', why we get 'Ifeoma doesn't write Jaja' (p. 300) instead of 'write to' and why Ifeoma says 'he has gotten' not 'he has got' (p. 181).

The novel also uses American spellings such as 'colored' for 'coloured' (p. 142), 'center' for 'centre' (p. 155), 'neighborhood' for 'neighbourhood' (p. 178), 'checks' for cheques (p. 297) — and many more examples.

Beneath the English narrative, most characters in *Purple Hibiscus* are speaking Igbo most of the time. It is the language that Kambili and Jaja use to each other and to Mama, for example. Ifeoma and her family speak it at home and with Father Amadi. Apart from Papa-Nnukwu (who has no education), most characters are bilingual.

Papa speaks mostly English because he wants to distance himself from his African roots and Kambili comments on it when he speaks Igbo. Note, however, that he carefully makes his accent more British when he speaks to white people (p. 46) and that it becomes overladen with Igbo when he is angry and out of control (p. 210).

Adichie continually reminds us that most conversations in *Purple Hibiscus* are in Igbo in two ways. First, she drops italicised Igbo words into direct speech, usually explaining, or unobtrusively making, their meaning clear as she goes.

Second, and more subtly, she uses expressions that sound quaint and odd in English because she wants to create a feeling that they have been translated from Igbo in which different turns of phrase are used. Examples of this technique include Jaja's polite question to Papa-Nnukwu, 'How is your body?' (p. 65) and Yewande Coker telling Papa in distress that one of her three children 'is still sucking my breast' (p. 37).

Text **focus**

Read carefully several times the passage from '"I was thinking about my father..."' (p. 268) to '...I could see my reflection in them' (p. 269).

- Apart from Father Amadi's longer speech about boarding school (top of p. 269), all the dialogue here is short and simple: 'Has he called?', 'Look at me, Kambili.' Beneath this, Adichie has layered a subtext in which Kambili is dreading the future, is worried about her relationship with her father and experiencing deep feelings for the kind, gentle, attractive Father Amadi.
- Kambili's feelings are mixed. On the one hand she is frightened by what will happen if or when she and Jaja go home and she has refused to speak to her father on the phone. In another way, she wants to please her father,

PHILIP ALLAN LITERATURE GUIDE **FOR GCSE**

to get his approval and make him smile: 'to hear his voice, to tell him what I had eaten and what I had prayed about'. She is surprised that perceptive Father Amadi understands this: 'It was not what I expected him to ask.'

- Adichie evokes a quiet closeness between Father Amadi and Kambili here, quite unlike anything the narrator has ever experienced with another human being. His tenderness is evoked by the adverbs: he speaks and acts 'gently' and 'carefully'.

- The closeness between Father Amadi and Kambili is physical too. They stand so close that their bellies almost touch and there is intimacy in his taking the flower from her finger and sliding it onto his own. She fantasises about embracing him.

- Adichie reminds us of Kambili's conditioning with the reference to the catechism. So used is Kambili to 'chanting the answer to a question' automatically that she instantly remembers an answer learned by heart and applies it to Father Amadi.

- At the end of the passage, Adichie breaks the atmosphere by making Kambili laugh in response to Father Amadi's botanical ignorance. The verb 'laughed' is repeated four times in three lines in the final paragraph. It is Adichie's way of showing that at this moment Kambili is happy, although it is rueful because she knows that Father Amadi is soon to leave the country.

Key quotation

That was the problem with our people, Papa told us, our priorities were wrong; we cared too much about huge church buildings and mighty statues. You would never see white people doing that.

(Kambili, p. 104)

Review your learning

(Answers on p. 93)

1 What sort of narrative is *Purple Hibiscus*?

2 In what part of which country is the entire novel set?

3 Why does Adichie use so many Igbo words?

4 How does Adichie make her imagery specifically African?

5 Find and list three examples of similes in *Purple Hibiscus* that are not mentioned in this chapter.

6 How does Adichie use language to develop character?

More interactive questions and answers online.

Tackling the assessments

- What sort of question will you have to answer in the exam?
- How can you plan your answer?
- What is the best way to start and finish your answers?
- How should you use quotations?

Your examining board: AQA

Purple Hibiscus is set by AQA (Assessments and Qualifications Alliance). It is assessed in Unit 1 Section B of Exploring Modern Texts: Exploring Cultures.

The work on *Purple Hibiscus* is the first half of a 1 hour 30 minute paper, so you have 45 minutes to spend on it.

This is an 'open text exam'. This means that you are expected to take your copy of the novel into the exam with you. It must, however, be a 'clean copy'. In other words, nothing must be handwritten on the pages of the novel and you are not allowed to take any notes into the exam room.

AQA sets only one compulsory task on *Purple Hibiscus*, so there is no choice of questions. The question set, which is in two parts, will refer you to a passage in the novel, a page or two in length.

You will be asked:

(a) to write about the detail in the passage and

(b) how the passage relates to the rest of the novel

Higher and foundation tier

Like all exam boards, AQA sets its English Literature GCSE exams at higher and foundation tier. If you take the higher-tier exam, you can get grades A*–D (with the possibility of an E). If you take the foundation-tier exam, you can get grades C–G. You and your teachers (and probably parents) will decide which is the more suitable level for you.

Higher-tier candidates are provided with the two-part question and are expected to work out for themselves how to structure an answer. If you are entered for the higher tier, you will be set tasks like this in the exam:

Read the passage which begins on p. 140 with 'Laughter always rang out…' and ends on p. 141 with '…ran out and into the toilet'.
(a) How does Adichie use the details in this passage to show the differences between Kambili's upbringing and Amaka's?
(b) How is the contrast between Kambili's home life and that of her cousins shown in the novel as a whole?

Foundation-tier candidates will be given similar tasks but with extra guidance. The bullet points below each question suggest an outline framework for the answer. For example:

Read the passage which begins on p. 140 with 'Laughter always rang out…' and ends on p. 141 with '…ran out and into the toilet'.
(a) What do you learn from this passage about the differences between Kambili's upbringing and Amaka's?
(b) How do we find out about the contrast between Kambili's home life and that of her cousins in the rest of the novel?
- Write about Ifeoma's home, Amaka's manner and how these things make Kambili feel.
- Write about how Chimamanda Ngozi Adichie, the author of *Purple Hibiscus*, shows us Papa's behaviour as a parent compared with Ifeoma's and other differences between the two households.

Grade *booster*

As a revision exercise, choose a passage from *Purple Hibiscus* of one to two pages. Set yourself, or a partner, a two-part question on it, including the bullet points you would expect to see if it were offered at foundation tier. This is a useful activity whichever tier you are entered for because it forces you to think analytically about the passage.

Tackling the tasks

Remember:
- English Literature does not have right and wrong answers.
- No two answers, even if they score the same marks, will contain exactly the same material.
- You can answer a question in more than one way and still score high marks.
- All your points must be supported by evidence (quotations or reference to events) from the novel.
- You must do more than retell the story: your job is to demonstrate your knowledge and understanding by commenting on the novel.
- Frequent use of the author's name will signal to the examiner that you are aware that the novel is something creative, designed to fulfil a writer's purpose(s).
- The examiner is interested in your response to *Purple Hibiscus* and what you think about it.

Planning your answers

Always work out what the question is asking you to do and make a plan before you begin. In an exam, when you are under time pressure, you will have to do this quickly. First, use a highlighter to make the key words in the question stand out, or underline them.

Then devise a plan for both parts of your answer — even two or three minutes spent making a plan will pay off. Your response will be better thought out, better shaped and you are less likely to miss out important points if you have noted them in your plan. This could make the difference between getting a C or D grade and a B, A or A*.

Since the question you are being asked is in two separate (but related) parts, it is probably better to think of them as two short essays.

Experiment with different sorts of plan and decide what works for you. Some people like diagrammatic plans. This usually means putting the key idea in a circle in the middle of the page and adding points for inclusion, linked to the key idea, around the outside. Alternatively, make a list and number the points.

Below is a two-part plan for the following question.

> Read the passage which begins on p. 167 with 'Papa Nnukwu was on a low wooden stool…' and ends on p. 169 with '…none of us did'.
> **(a)** How does Adichie use the details in this passage to show Papa-Nnukwu's religion and Kambili's reaction to it?
> **(b)** How are the tensions between Roman Catholic Christianity and other religions shown in the novel as a whole?

1 Intro: K watching silently, unseen by PN in early morning, If. wants her to see religious similarities
2 PN's devout manner
3 People PN prays for
4 K's detailed observation of PN's appearance
5 Comparison of PN praying with what K is used to
6 Conc: Adichie reinforces sense of Kambili's astonishment with the detailed account of what she saw and heard

1 Intro: v strict Roman Catholicism, via Papa, dominates K's life
2 PN (& old man who tries to visit at Abba) represents traditional African religion which Papa has rejected
3 Differences between F. Amadi and F. Benedict
4 Aunty I's cheerful moderate Catholicism

5 P's hatred of other forms of Christianity

6 Conc: Adichie presents the religious tensions partly as a theme to explore; also part of characterisation

Always 'frame' each part of your answer with an introduction and a conclusion, however brief. You are unlikely to be able to make more than four or five main points in each of your answers in the time available to you in the exam.

Try to plan your time carefully so that you always complete your answer.

The sample plan above is, of course, not the only way that this question could be answered. As a revision exercise, devise a plan of your own for a different answer to this question. In part (b), you might include, for example:

- Mama's religious attitudes and behaviour
- the presentation of Sister Lucy, the nun who tutors Kambili in hospital
- Jaja's growing awareness that Roman Catholicism, as enforced by his father, may not be how he, Jaja, wants to live

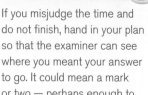

Grade **booster**

If you misjudge the time and do not finish, hand in your plan so that the examiner can see where you meant your answer to go. It could mean a mark or two — perhaps enough to push your work into the next grade.

Essay openings

You will get no marks for copying the question in your opening sentence or paragraph. Instead, your introduction might:

- indicate how you are going to tackle the question
- interpret the question — say what you think it means
- comment on something that is in the question
- make a clear statement which can be quite short

The examiner's aim is to seek out the mark-scoring parts of your answer. You will score marks for making informed analytical comments. Do not waste your limited time writing anything else.

Below are three possible introductions for an answer to part (a) of the question above relating to pp. 167–69:

- The details in this passage fall into three categories: what Kambili notices about Papa Nnukwu's appearance in the dawn; what she hears him say in his prayers; her thoughts and reflections. Each will be considered in turn.
- The most striking thing about this passage is that, almost for the first time, Kambili realises that Papa-Nnukwu's traditionalist religion is not so different from her own. Adichie drives this home in her use of details.
- In the quiet dawn light, the homely strangeness of Papa Nnukwu's near-nakedness seems quite unlike anything Kambili has seen before and she is astonished to hear the details of her grandfather's prayers.

Text focus

Read carefully several times the passage which begins on p. 101 with 'Papa's white shirt…' and ends on p. 102 with '…swished through the air'.

- The first paragraph is almost motionless, like a 'freeze frame' in a film. Papa stands still in his smart white church shirt and Kambili has time to notice how overweight he is. He has arrived silently. No one speaks. It is Adichie's dramatic way of presenting the shock of the moment at which Mama, Kambili and Jaja are 'caught' doing something they know Papa will be angry about.
- Although it is Kambili who is eating the cereal and breaking the strict pre-mass rule about fasting, both Mama and Jaja try to take the blame to protect her. This pattern is repeated several times during the novel, most obviously at the end when Jaja goes to prison for murder to save his mother.
- Papa, who speaks English when he is under control — because he regards it as the language of education and civilisation — is shown to be losing control: 'The Igbo words burst out of Papa's mouth.'
- The belt unbuckling is slow, deliberate and ominous. Kambili has time to notice that it is 'heavy', that it is 'made of layers of brown leather' and that it has 'a sedate leather-covered buckle'.
- Papa, who tries so hard to reject his African background, but fails, reminds Kambili of a Fulani nomad driving cattle. It is a comparison that helps to remind us that Papa is a first-generation Christian and failing to adopt the European ways he claims to admire so much.
- This incident is linked, later in the novel, to other incidents of Papa's violence towards his children, such as the foot scalding and the beating that puts Kambili in hospital. Although he often hits his wife in private, this is the only time we see her being struck in front of her children — treated exactly as they are.
- Adichie evokes Papa's way of speaking with words like 'burst' and 'muttering' as he struggles to gain or regain control of three people who have disobeyed him. He thinks he is fighting evil: 'Has the devil asked you all to go on errands for him?', 'Has the devil built a tent in my house?', 'muttering that the devil would not win'. In fact, he is angry because his rules have been broken.
- Kambili, Jaja and Mama are presented as being so conditioned to submitting that, apart from Mama who 'raised her hands as it landed on her upper arm', none of them attempt to avoid the attack: 'We did not move more than two steps away from the leather belt that swished through the air.'

Essay endings

You will get no extra marks for repeating in your conclusion something that you have said already. In your conclusion, you might:

● summarise your arguments and draw them together in a new way
● make a new point which you have deliberately held back for the ending
● try to be 'punchy' so that there is a sense of an answer that has been finished rather than just tailing off

Below are three possible conclusions for the answer to part (b) of a question based on pp. 167–69 of *Purple Hibiscus*.

● I think, and I have tried to show, that Adichie respects Roman Catholic Christianity, which can be loving and tolerant. That is why she presents Ifeoma's family and Father Amadi as a contrast to Kambili's own family and Papa's bigotry.

● *Purple Hibiscus* presents four sorts of religion and their effects on people, as I have tried to show here: strict Roman Catholicism (Papa), gentle Roman Catholicism (Father Amadi), other forms of Christianity (disparagingly mentioned occasionally by Papa) and traditional African ancestor worship (Papa-Nnukwu). It is the tensions between these four which underpin the novel's plot, characterisation and themes.

● Papa-Nnukwu, as we have seen, represents in *Purple Hibiscus* the traditionalist African religion which Christian missionaries have tried, but failed, to wipe out. It can sit alongside Christianity, as it does in Ifeoma's household, or it can be a cause of deep unhappiness and tension, as it is in Kambili's home.

> **Key quotation**
>
> I wanted to go over and touch Papa-Nnukwu, touch the white tufts of hair that Amaka had oiled, smooth the wrinkled skin of his chest. But I would not. Papa would be outraged.
>
> (Kambili, p. 184)

> **Key quotation**
>
> Then I heard Amaka's sobbing. It was loud and throaty; she laughed the way she cried. She had not learned the art of silent crying; she had not needed to.
>
> (Kambili, p. 185)

> **Key quotation**
>
> 'It's good to see you are yourself again,' Father Amadi said, looking me over, as if to see if I was all there. I smiled. He motioned me to stand up for a hug. His body touching mine was tense and delicious.
>
> (Kambili, p. 221)

Grade *booster*

Use strong and carefully chosen verbs in your answers to describe what Adichie is doing. For example, 'By …, the author suggests/ depicts/evokes/ hints/conveys/questions/asks/presents/offers/clarifies/implies…'. This will help to make your writing more self-assured and analytical. It is analysis which examiners are looking for in A*–C answers.

Grade *focus*

How does Adichie show the gradual change in Jaja?

Grades A*–C points	Grades D–G points
While Kambili and Jaja are staying in Ifeoma's flat, Adichie has Kambili notice the muscles in Jaja's arms and hair on his chest. The reader is made aware that Jaja is physically no longer the child that Papa wants him to be.	Jaja has grown up. He has strong muscles and hairs on his chest.
The rebellion on Palm Sunday is crucial to the structure of the novel and, since it opens *Purple Hibiscus*, the reader is never allowed to forget that Jaja at 17 is no longer the compliant, unquestioning child prepared to obey Papa in everything.	Jaja won't take communion on Palm Sunday as his father has always made him do. He is learning to stand up for himself.
Jaja, emboldened by open and free conversations in Ifeoma's home, asks for the key to his bedroom in Enugu. It is the beginning of his establishing his own independence. Adichie makes it clear that Papa also knows he has lost because when Jaja barricades himself into his bedroom with a piece of furniture, Kambili notices that Papa does not force his way in.	Jaja asks Papa for his bedroom key. Papa thinks Jaja wants to masturbate and says no, so Jaja puts something across his door to keep Papa out.

Using evidence in essays

Just as scientists provide evidence to back up their theories, you need to provide evidence to back up the points you make in your essay. All the evidence you require lies within the covers of *Purple Hibiscus*.

There are two sorts of evidence: quotations and general references to the text (events, characters etc.).

Quotations of exact words written in the novel

Look for short phrases that illustrate your point and weave them into your sentences. Always remember to include quotation marks. You should not need to quote more than one sentence at a time. Aim to work at least eight direct quotations into an exam answer. Structure your sentences as in these examples:

- Kevin, 'our driver' who has 'a dagger-shape scar' on his neck, is usually a silent presence but he is supportive of Papa, and Kambili and Mama find him disconcerting which is why, after Papa's death, Mama dismisses him.

- Adichie makes clear the difference between 'traditionalist' Pagan and Christian rituals in Kambili's account of the mmuo figure with its mask consisting of 'a real, grimacing human skull with sunken eye sockets'.
- Although we warm to the 'exuberant, fearless, loud, larger than life' Ifeoma and she is kind to Kambili, she is unable to protect her niece from abuse at home.

General references to the text

For example, you might mention, without quoting directly:

- the occasion when Kambili is told about Ade Coker's death by letter bomb and she imagines the scene at the breakfast table in the Coker household
- the presentation of the gentle-voiced Celestine who becomes driver to Kambili and Mama after Papa's death
- the sequence of events that leads to Ifeoma's decision to leave Nigeria and take her family to the USA

Writing examination answers

Five dos

- Write as fully as you can but be selective and focus on detail.
- Make a quick plan before you start. Aim to make five or six key points and manage your time carefully — which includes leaving yourself a few minutes at the end to reread your work.
- Back up your statements with evidence from the novel.
- Spell and punctuate accurately, especially the names of characters and places in the novel.
- Use formal English and avoid slang and colloquialisms.

Five don'ts

- Don't retell the story.
- Don't waste your time writing out long quotations that are not grafted tightly into your arguments.
- Don't begin sentences or paragraphs with 'The above quotation shows…'
- Don't try to write everything you know about *Purple Hibiscus*.
- Don't confuse Chimamanda Ngozi Adichie, the author of *Purple Hibiscus*, with Kambili, her fictional narrator.

> **Pause for thought**
>
> How do you feel about *Purple Hibiscus* being examined only by a single passage-based question? Would you prefer to have written an essay, and if so why?

Review your learning

(Answers on p. 93)

1. Which exam board sets *Purple Hibiscus*?
2. What is the main difference between higher- and foundation-tier questions?
3. What form will your examination question take?
4. What two sorts of evidence can you use in your exam answer?
5. How will you set about planning your answer?
6. What might you include in an answer's a) introduction and b) conclusion?

More interactive questions and answers online.

Assessment Objectives and skills

- **What are Assessment Objectives?**
- **What do you have to include in your answers?**
- **How important are presentation matters such as spelling and punctuation?**
- **How do you achieve an A* answer?**

All GCSE examinations are pinned to specific areas of learning which the examiners want to be sure that candidates have mastered. These are known as Assessment Objectives, or AOs.

Think of AOs as darts board-like targets or as targets on a shooting range. The examiner is watching the target, you aim for it. You get marks if you hit it, but not if you do not — and, in general, the more direct your hit, the more marks you are likely to get.

There are four AOs for GCSE English Literature but only three that relate to your work on *Purple Hibiscus*. You cannot, of course, divide learning of this sort into neat, self-contained chunks, so the AOs overlap.

You are required to show in your answer that you can:

- **AO1**: respond to texts critically and imaginatively; select and evaluate relevant textual detail to illustrate and support interpretations
- **AO2**: explain how language, structure and form contribute to writers' presentation of ideas, themes and settings
- **AO4**: relate texts to their social, cultural and historical contexts; explain how texts have been influential and significant to self and other readers in different contexts and at different times

NB: AO3 is tested elsewhere in the exam but does not relate to *Purple Hibiscus*.

So what do these rather complicated AO statements actually mean, and what are examiners really looking for?

AO1

You must show that you have read the book carefully and thought about it from a number of angles. Bear in mind the two terms 'imaginatively' and 'critically':

- First, you need to have travelled to Enugu, Nsukka and Abba in your mind, considered how Kambili, Papa and other characters must have felt, and thought carefully about why. That is imaginative reading. But of course, to meet this AO, not only do you have to read imaginatively, you also have to be able to write about your reading in order to demonstrate its imaginativeness.
- Critical reading is a different skill. It involves being aware of *why* Adichie makes the decisions that she does. Why, for instance, does she make Kambili the narrator and not Jaja or Papa? Would it have been a better or worse novel if she had told the story differently? What use does she make of 'lesser characters' such as Obiora, Father Benedict and Ade Coker? Why are they in the novel and what is their purpose? Some answers to these questions are suggested in earlier sections of this guide. If you show that you are aware of such questions, and are able to offer some ideas to answer them in your exam essays, you will be demonstrating 'critical' reading and meeting the AO1 target.

One way of making sure that you write 'critically' is to use the author's name or to refer to her as often as you can. Make statements beginning, for instance:

- Chimamanda Ngozi Adichie makes us aware…
- Adichie presents…
- The author makes it clear that…
- Adichie makes Kambili say…
- Adichie tells us through Kambili…
- Chimamanda Ngozi Adichie wants to show the reader that…

Remember — and this is the second part of AO1 — that every point (or 'interpretation') you make must be supported with 'relevant textual detail'. This means that you use brief quotations or you refer to incidents in the text as evidence to support what you are saying.

AO2

This AO requires you to show that you understand not just what Adichie has written in *Purple Hibiscus* but how she has used her writer's tools. Like all authors, Adichie has used language precisely for specific purposes and she has chosen to shape her novel to tell her story in a particular way. 'Language, structure and form' covers things such as:

- Adichie's use of an invisible adult narrator looking back on her childhood and therefore able to use reflective language (see p. 59).
- Adichie's use of rather un-English expressions — and Igbo words — to suggest that most of the dialogue is translated from another language.

To meet AO2, you also need to show how Adichie uses these 'tools' to tell her story and to convey the messages she wants to get across to the reader. This is what is meant by her 'presentation of ideas, themes and settings'.

> **Key quotation**
>
> I did not know that Papa-Nnukwu liked to go on and on. I did not even know that he told stories.
>
> (Kambili, p. 72)

> **Key quotation**
>
> '...when Papa-Nnukwu did his itu-nzu, his declaration of innocence, in the morning, it was the same as our saying the rosary.'
>
> (Kambili reporting Ifeoma's comment, p. 166)

Text focus

Read carefully several times the passage which begins 'After lunch I asked Amaka...' (p. 121) and ends '...but I was not sure what for' (p. 122).

- Adichie carefully highlights the physical differences here between the basic, small lavatory which cannot be flushed often and the large arrangement Kambili is used to with 'soft rugs' and a 'furry cover for the toilet seat'.
- Adichie uses bleak language to describe the lavatory: 'narrow', 'empty', 'limply'.
- The straightforward, factual word 'urinated' sounds odd in English because it is rarely used within families in Britain where some sort of euphemism is usual. This is, almost certainly, a translation of what would have been said in Igbo. The same probably applies to the expression 'ease myself'.
- This passage runs mostly on its dialogue, which flows along like a play and without the need to slow the pace by laboriously explaining who is speaking as Kambili asks Ifeoma about the water.
- Adichie shows us Amaka's bitterness through what she says sharply and through her decisive dismissiveness as she walks to the refrigerator and pours a glass of water.
- Notice Ifeoma's sensitivity in hearing what Amaka says and reprimanding her for her tone — promptly accepted by Amaka, who knows that she is in the wrong.
- Kambili, meanwhile, is feeling so uncomfortable that she wants to disappear.

AO4

Examining the context of a novel involves seeing the situation it presents in comparison with other situations at other times and in other places. This is discussed in detail in the *Context* section of this guide.

In brief, the historical context of *Purple Hibiscus* is that it is set in the early 1990s in south eastern Nigeria. A military coup is making life difficult for anyone who objects to military dictatorship. Ade Coker is killed for expressing a view and Ifeoma loses her job for being critical. Papa also objects but he is wealthy and powerful enough to escape censure, although Kambili is often frightened that he too will be targeted. When she is told that he is dead (pp. 286–87), her first thought is that a letter bomb has killed him, just like Ade Coker.

At the same time, Papa and Ifeoma — both Roman Catholics — are the result of missionary education, a direct consequence of Nigeria's having been a British colony (which is another strand of historical context).

The novel's main social context is its family settings. Most of the novel is set either in one of Kambili's homes or at Ifeoma's, with one episode at Papa-Nnukwu's when Kambili and Jaja visit him. Alongside that are brief trips to church, to the market, to the stadium with Father Amadi, to school, trips with Ifeoma and to the prison at the end of the novel.

Look carefully at the community at Abba, where Papa is given the title of '*omelora*' (pp. 55–103). He lives in a palatial house which is used for only a week once a year at Christmas. He is head of a large '*umunna*' — a clan, community or, loosely, an extended family. There is some communal cooking and presentation of senior people, but Papa and his family eat privately.

Purple Hibiscus's cultural context comes at several levels. Nigeria is influenced by its colonial past. Its people aspire to the education and comfortable life which is usual in Europe and its richest people (like Papa in the novel) do have these things.

This is contrasted with the everyday life of Africans such as Papa-Nnukwu who have largely resisted getting caught up in European culture. Papa Nnukwu has had no education, cannot read or write and does not speak English, but of course he buys things from the store when he can afford it and rides in Ifeoma's car.

At family level, there is the culture of the tight Roman Catholic culture of the community of St Agnes Church in Enugu (funded largely by Papa), with its white priest Father Benedict. The strict bigotry of Kambili's home ruled by Papa is an extreme example of this culture.

This is compared with the more liberal Christian culture of Ifeoma's home, where independent thought and discussion are encouraged. Note, too, how Father Amadi befriends the poor African boys and plays football with them at the stadium — a practical example of Christian charity.

Of course, these three aspects of context — social, cultural and historical — are closely related to each other and there is a lot of overlap. The important thing to remember is that you have to bear the context in mind as you read, study and write about *Purple Hibiscus*. You cannot make sense of the novel without it.

When you are writing, it makes sense occasionally to use the words 'social context', 'cultural context' and 'historical context', or something similar, to show the examiner that you are fulfilling AO4.

Quality of written communication

In addition to the three AOs, your work on *Purple Hibiscus* will also be marked by AQA for its quality of written communication (QWC). Examiners expect you to:

- ensure that what you write is legible and that spelling, punctuation and grammar are accurate so that meaning is clear
- select and use a form and style of writing appropriate to purpose and to complex subject matter
- organise your information clearly and coherently, using specialist vocabulary when relevant

Grade *focus*

Write about Adichie's style.

Grades A*–C points	Grades D–G points
Adichie uses Kambili as a first-person narrator. This gives *Purple Hibiscus* an immediacy and makes all the events described seem plausible because they are presented as if by a witness.	Kambili tells the story.
Because most of her characters speak in Igbo most of the time, Adichie sprinkles her text with Igbo words so that the reader never forgets which language is being spoken. She also uses slightly strange expressions in English, such as 'I do not know if my head is correct' (p. 248), to convey a sense of another language.	Chimamanda Ngozi Adichie uses a lot of Igbo words because her story is set in Nigeria.
Adichie's characters, especially Kambili, often make colourful comparisons which contribute to the Nigerian atmosphere. For example, Kambili compares Papa's face to a coconut (p. 25) and Papa Nnukwu's nipples to dark raisins (p. 169).	The author sometimes describes things by using comparisons. Papa Nnukwu's nipples are like raisins (p. 169).

How to get an A* grade

To get an A* grade, you must:

- answer the question fully or do whatever the task asks you to do
- construct a clear argument or line of reasoning
- make good use of frequent, relevant short quotations within your sentences
- shape your answer by planning it with an introduction and conclusion
- express your ideas in good English
- write clearly with precision and in an appropriate tone
- spell and punctuate accurately

Review your learning

(Answers on p. 94)

1 What are Assessment Objectives or AOs?

2 How many AOs relate to your work on *Purple Hibiscus*?

3 What, in brief, are these AOs?

4 What is QWC?

5 What are the main differences between a grade C answer and an A* answer?

6 What must you do to get an A*?

 More interactive questions and answers online.

Sample essays

Question 1

Read the passage which begins with 'Papa-Nnukwu was sitting on a low stool…' (p. 64) and ends with '…it will be in my hands' (p. 65).

(a) How does Adichie use details in this passage to present the relationship between Papa-Nnukwu and his grandchildren?

(b) How is the conflict between the beliefs of Papa-Nnukwu and those of Papa shown in the novel as a whole?

Grade-A* answer

(a) By drawing attention to Papa Nnukwu's poverty-stricken appearance (the old stained vest and the wrapper are the first things Kambili notices), Adichie makes us aware that the children do not see their grandfather very often.**1 (AO2)** Kambili finds him faintly repellent, too, as she notices 'the strong, unpleasant smell of cassava that clung to him'. We are also seeing another side of Nigeria — the poverty of the ordinary, uneducated people, whose lives at this time, under a military dictatorship, are very different from Kambili's and Jaja's. **(AO4)**

1 Clear, confident opening

It is also made clear that the children do not often spend time with Papa-Nnukwu because Kambili has difficulty following his 'ancient' Igbo dialect as it is very different from her own Igbo, which has 'anglicised inflections'.**2 (AO3)** Kambili and Jaja are products of the same European education which shaped Papa's extreme views and means that they all speak English bilingually alongside Igbo.

2 Neat use of appropriate 'woven in' quotations

The children are not allowed (by Papa) to accept food and drink from Papa-Nnukwu, who is not a Christian. **(AO4)** He knows this and is faintly amused by it. He offers refreshment, knows they will refuse and 'his eyes twinkled with mischief'. Adichie wants the reader to know that this conversation takes place each time Kambili and Jaja visit. **(AO2)**

The very formal way in which Jaja and Kambili speak to the old man — addressing him as 'sir' and making very polite, rather forced conversation — also indicates, at this early stage of the novel, that they do not spend much time with him. **(AO2)**

In contrast, Adichie presents Papa-Nnukwu as quite a relaxed old man ('the easy way…'), pleased to see his grandchildren and not bitter about the estrangement from his son. He teases Kambili, for example, about her womanliness: 'a ripe *agbogho*'. He smiles a lot, despite increasing blindness in one eye and various ailments for which his daughter cannot always afford to bring medicine. **(AO1)**

At the beginning of the novel, Kambili and Jaja hardly know their grandfather because they are allowed to visit him only once a year for a very stilted 15 minutes as there is a deep rift between Papa-Nnukwu and his extremist Roman Catholic son. Adichie uses this passage to introduce this strand in the novel.**3 (AO2)**

3 Good link with one of the main themes of the novel

(b) For Papa, Papa-Nnukwu (like the old man who tries to visit at Abba and is ruthlessly and rudely evicted) represents everything about the old Nigerian ways which he has fiercely tried to reject. **(AO1, AO4)** Papa frequently uses terms such as 'pagan', 'heathen' and 'ancestor worship' and Adichie has him remind Kambili that he was educated at St Gregory's and worked to pay his own school fees because 'My father spent his time worshipping gods of wood and stone.'**4** **(AO2, AO4)**

4 Strong awareness of cultural context

Gradually, as the novel unfolds, because of the relationship with Aunty Ifeoma, Kambili and Jaja spend more time with Papa-Nnukwu. They learn, for example, that he is wise and tells good stories (pp. 157–61). They find he is rueful but accepting of Papa's rejection (p. 84) and they marvel at the relaxed way their cousins banter lovingly but respectfully with their grandfather. **(AO1)** Kambili is also surprised at the pleasant and tolerant way in which Father Amadi speaks to the old man, having helped Ifeoma to bring him to Nsukka. This is a very different style of family life and religious outlook from what they are used to. Adichie uses it to show just how extreme and unreasonable Papa's way of life and domination of his family really is.**5 (AO2)**

5 Sophisticated grasp of Adichie's narrative technique

Adichie has Kambili observing Papa-Nnukwu at morning prayer (pp. 167–69) and she is surprised by the gentle goodness of his 'heathen' prayers, especially when he prays for his son. Papa-Nnukwu is being used to show that traditional African religion is not so different in its intentions from Christianity. **(AO4)** There need not be, in fact, the huge rift between Papa's views and Papa Nnukwu's that there is, at least as far as Papa is concerned. **(AO2)**

When Papa-Nnukwu dies, Ifeoma and her children are deeply saddened. He was a very important part of their lives. Papa, however (unlike Mama when he tells her the news), shows no grief. **(AO1)** Rather, he berates his sister for not bringing in a Catholic priest to perform the last rites ('extreme unction'). Although Papa pays generously for his father's funeral, he is angry with Ifeoma for refusing to hold a Catholic funeral, saying, 'I cannot participate in a pagan funeral.' The difference between his bigotry and Ifeoma's humane tolerance (and unconditional love for her father) is made very clear here. **(AO2)**

Papa immediately removes his children from Ifeoma's home. When they get home, he punishes them for not telling him that Papa-Nnukwu was in Ifeoma's flat by scalding their feet with water from a kettle so that they know what hellfire feels like. 'This is what you do to yourself when you walk into sin. You burn your feet,' he tells Kambili (p. 194). **(AO1)** Adichie uses incidents like this — one of the most horrifying in *Purple Hibiscus* because Papa is calm and deliberate rather than angry — to show us more of Papa's extremism, which is so different from his late father's rueful but amused tolerance of the differences between himself and Papa.**6 (AO2)**

6 Well-chosen vocabulary, used accurately and incisively

This well-reasoned, articulate answer analyses the passage in depth, looks well beyond it in (b) and draws very insightful conclusions with plenty of focus on narrative technique and cultural dimensions.

Grade-C answer

(a) Papa Nnukwu is poor. He wears an old stained vest and a wrapper. Kambili doesn't like the way he smells either: 'the strong unplesent**1** smell of cassava that clung to him'.**2 (AO1)**

1 Spelling error

2 Simple but useful 'introduction'

It's obvious that the children don't see Papa-Nnukwu very often because Kambili finds it hard to follow what he says. **(AO2)**

Kambili and her brother can't take food and stuff from Papa-Nnukwu cos**3** he's a heathen. **(AO4)** He knows this and thinks its**4** quite funny so his eyes twinkle.

3 Inappropriately informal

4 Grammatical error

They don't speak to him like a granddad. They call him 'sir' and it's all very polite. That shows they don't spend much time with him too. **(AO2)**

In contrast Adichie presents Papa-Nnukwu as being quite laid back.**3** He does things in 'the easy way'. He's pleased to see his grandkids.**3** He tells Kambili she's growing up. The old man doesn't seem bitter that his son won't talk to him. **(AO1)**

At the begining**1** of the novel Kambili and Jaja hardly know their grandfather. That's because their father is a strict Catholic. In this passage Adichie introduces this idea in the novel.**5 (AO2)**

5 Some awareness of Adichie's storytelling method

(b) For Papa, Papa-Nnukwu sums up everything about the old Nigerian ways**6** which he doesn't like. Papa uses words such as 'pagan', 'heathen' and 'ancestor worship'. He tells Kambili that he had to work to pay his own school fees because 'My father spent his time worshipping gods of wood and stone.' **(AO4)**

6 Some awareness of cultural factors

Later on Kambili is surprised how chatty and friendly her cousins are with Papa-Nnukwu. She's also gobsmacked**3** at how nice Father Amadi (Catholic preist**1**) is to the old man. It shows up how strict and unreasonable Papa is in her own home.**5 (AO2)**

Kambili watches Papa-Nnukwu say his morning prayers. He's quite kind and gentle and even prays for Papa. It's a bit like Kambili's own prayers. **(AO1)**

Then Papa-Nnukwu dies. Ifeoma and her children are terribly upset. But Papa doesn't seem bothered.**3** He just goes on about how**3** Ifeoma should of**4** got a Catholic priest in to convert the old man on his deathbed. But he pays for the funeral (although he won't go to it) so that Ifeoma can get a lot of goats for **7** Some attempt at analysis   guests to eat. The author is trying to say that Ifeoma is kinder than Papa.**7 (AO2)**

After all that Papa, whose**4** furious, takes his kids**3** home. Then he pours boiling water on their feet because they didn't tell him that their grandfather had come to stay. **(AO1)**

This bit of the story really shows you**5** what a strict man with wayout**3** views Papa is. He isn't a bit like his own father what's**3,4** just died. **(AO1)**

This answer explores the passage in some detail and in (b) some of the issues beyond it. It shows some understanding of cultural differences and narrative technique. However, it is not particularly well expressed and there are errors in the English.

Question 2

> Read the passage which begins with '"What is that? Have you all converted…"' and ends with '…and slipped away into quiet'
> (pp. 209–11).
> **(a)** How does Adichie use the details in this passage to show the violent side of Papa's personality?
> **(b)** How are the different facets of Papa's complex personality shown and developed in the rest of the novel?

Grade-A* answer

1 Clear, effective introduction

(a) This passage opens with Kambili claiming ownership of Amaka's painting of Papa-Nnukwu. She is contradicting Jaja who, as usual, has tried to take the blame in order to save Kambili from Papa's anger. **(AO1)** The simple, truthful statement 'It's mine' is a sign that she — like her brother — is getting stronger.**1**

2 High-level critical insight into Adichie's choice of language, structure and form

The contradiction is repeated a few lines on when both Kambili and Jaja claim to have brought the painting into the house and Adichie presents Kambili**2** saying clearly to herself, 'If only Jaja would look at me, I would ask him not to blame himself.' **(AO2)**

This is one of the occasions in the novel — the most violent of all — when Papa completely loses his temper because his will is being crossed and he is beginning to lose control of his children. **(AO1)** First, frighteningly, he sways, not like someone overcome at a religious ceremony, but like 'a bottle of Coke that burst into violent foam when you opened it'**3**. The simile Adichie gives Kambili**2** is unerringly apt here because her father is about to erupt in terrible temper. **(AO2)**

3 Short, relevant quotations used in support of points

Then he destroys the painting by ripping it into small pieces and it becomes, for Kambili, a symbol of 'something lost, something I had never had, would never have',**3 (AO1)** by which she means the happy relationship with her grandfather that her cousins enjoyed and the warmth of extended tolerant family. The latter is denied her because of her father's personality and his rejection of his own family roots. **(AO4)**

Trying to gather up the paper fragments, shrieking 'No!' at her father and refusing to get up from the floor is, in a sense, a defiance of Papa. **(AO2)** In the past, she has submitted to his orders and decisions. It is her disobedience which triggers the kicking, including injuring her with the buckles on his slippers which 'stung like bites from giant mosquitoes'**3** — one of Adichie's cleverly chosen images for a narrator who has grown up in Africa. **(AO2)** At the same time, Papa's English is slipping into Igbo, as it always does when he is out of control.**4 (AO4)** His behaviour is, ironically, as horrifyingly unreasonable as anything done by the military dictators ruling Nigeria that he works so hard at despising. **(AO4)**

4 Reasoned argument developing

Adichie gives Kambili — who eventually passes out — some well-observed mental illusions as she thinks about music and the way it often starts quietly and builds up. **(AO2)** She reflects on the source of the attack, which becomes even more frenzied. Kambili lies curled in the foetal position while Papa kicks, slaps and strikes her with his slippers and belt. **(AO1)**

By showing Papa, who is beside himself with anger and remorse about the death of his editor Ade Coker, in this frenzied, angry attack which sends his daughter to hospital for several weeks, Adichie is showing the reader — and Mama — that something really has to be done to ensure that the children are permanently safe from their father.**2 (AO2)**

(b) Papa can be very violent and quite easily loses control of himself, as this passage shows. On the other hand, he is regarded as a philanthropist, funds St Agnes Church in Enugu, pays school fees for over a hundred children, gives money away to beggars and other poor people every time he goes out and has won an award from the publication *Amnesty World*. **(AO1)** He also helps the Coker family when Ade is imprisoned and later when he is killed, and he is held in great regard by most of his *ummuna* in Abba. Adichie paints a distinctive social context in these details and carefully places Papa within it.**1 (AO4)**

Adichie includes all these details in Kambili's account **(AO2)** because she is creating and developing a complex character of many facets, not just a man who treats his wife and children as possessions he can 'punish' as he chooses. He is not all bad, by any means.

At the same time, she shows us several instances of Papa's treatment of his own family, shocking to the reader. He attacks them with a belt for breaking the fast before communion, he burns Kambili's and Jaja's feet for withholding information and, as described in the passage discussed in this question, he almost kills Kambili. When Jaja was ten years old, Papa deliberately and permanently mutilated the little finger on his left hand and he has beaten his wife so often that she has miscarried every child she has conceived in the 15 years since Kambili was born. **(AO1)**

Despite this, Kambili — wary of him as she is — also loves her father. She enjoys climbing on his knee and taking 'love sips'**3** from his tea cup and loves to see him smile. She is distressed to see him ill, his face 'swollen, oily discoloured'**3** when he begins to succumb to the cumulative effects of Mama's poison. **(AO1)**

Beneath Papa's piety, Adichie wants us to see a man who is at war with himself.**4** **(AO2)** He condemns pride as a sin but is clearly proud of his own achievements (when he is feted in church as a donor, for instance). He is greedy, too. Kambili comments several times on his being fat. His extreme, humourless religiosity is partly a reaction to his own upbringing, which he is determined not to slip back towards in any way and which is why he does not approve of Igbo songs in church. Yet, when he loses his temper (as in this passage), it is angry Igbo, the language of his childhood, which bursts out of him. **(AO1)**

The novel opens with, and is structured around**2**, Papa's hurling a religious book across the room in anger and breaking Mama's ornaments on Palm Sunday. Compared with what happens elsewhere in the novel, this does not seem especially serious. However, when we realise, much later in the novel, that this is after the serious attack on Kambili and that Mama is already poisoning him, we understand the significance of the Palm Sunday event and that Papa's power is, by then, gone. **(AO1)**

Papa is a tragic figure. **(AO1)** His intolerance and temper are fatal flaws in his character.**4** He will never change, which is why he has to die to give Kambili, Jaja and Mama some hope of a peaceful future, although the ending of the novel is ambiguous and one senses that Adichie wants us to suspect that none of them will ever fully recover from the mental damage Papa has done them. **(AO2)**

This very well-expressed and structured answer, in flawless English, deals with both parts of the question clearly and logically, with ample textual reference. It shows highly developed understanding of the context of Adichie's writing and the techniques she uses to tell her story.

Grade-C answer

(a) This passage starts with Kambili saying that Amaka's painting of Papa-Nnukwu belongs to her.**1** She says 'It's mine.' She says that because Jaja tries to make out**2** it's his. **(AO1)**

It happens again when both Kambili and Jaja claim to have brought the painting into the house. Kambili says to herself 'If only Jaja would look at me, I would ask him not to blame himself.'

This is one of the times in the novel **(AO2)** when Papa completely loses it**2** because his children are disobaying**3** him. First he sways 'like a bottle of Coke that burst into violent foam when you opened it'.**4** Kambili means that he's gonna**2** lose his temper. **(AO1)**

Then he rips the painting into small pieces — 'something lost, something I had never had, would never have'.**5**

Kambili tries to gather up the paper fragments, shrieking 'No!' at her father. She doesn't get off the floor when he tells her too**6** so he starts kicking her and the buckles on his slippers 'stung like bites from giant mosquitoes'.**4** Kambili thinks of mosquitoes because she lives in Africa.**7** **(AO4)** Papa forgets to speak English because he's so angry. **(AO2)**

Kambili begins to drift off as her dad gets more violent. She curls up and thinks about music. Papa kicks, slaps and strikes her with his belt. **(AO1)**

Papa is in a state cos**2** he thinks it was his fault that the editor of his newspaper was killed. But he obveeusly**3** has to be sorted out**2**, which is why, a bit later, Mama kills him. **(AO2)**

(b) Papa can be very violent and quite easily loses control of himself, as this passage shows. **(AO2)**

But he is also a good man in other ways. He gives lots of money to his church and he pays school fees for lots of poor children. **(AO1)** He also gives money to beggars and has won a newspaper prize.**8**

Adichie makes Kambili say all this **(AO2)** because she is creating and developing a complicated person with a good side and a bad.**9**

But he's awful to his family. **(AO1)** He hits them with a belt for breaking a church rule and he burns Kambili's and Jaja's feet for not telling him stuff.**2** When Jaja was ten years old, Papa broke his finger on purpose and he hits his wife so often that she keeps losing babies.**8** **(AO2)**

But Kambili loves him as well as being scared. **(AO1)** She likes to sit on his knee and drink from his tea cup and she likes it when he praises her. She loves to see

1 Clear introduction

2 Expression too colloquial for a formal English Literature assessment answer

3 Spelling error

4 Good use of quotation

5 'Dangling' quotation (not linked to a point)

6 Grammatical error

7 Shows awareness of context

8 Well-chosen examples

9 Shows awareness that Kambili and Papa are characters (and a narrator in the case of Kambili) constructed by the author

him smile. She's upset to see his face 'swollen, oily discoloured'**4** when he gets ill because of the poison. **(AO2)**

He's very religious, but Papa doesn't always follow the rules properly. He says its**6** wrong to be proud but he likes it when they say nice things about him at church. He is greedy too and Kambili hint's**6** he's a bit fat. **(AO1)**

He doesn't have any sense of humour and tries all the time to be European in his ways because he thinks British is best. That's because the British used to rule Nigeria.**7 (AO4)**

Papa is like a tragic hero. He has something deeply wrong inside and he isn't going to change. That is why in the end Mama takes action and kills him. **(AO1)**

This answer, which is quite well expressed in places, shows overall understanding of what the question is about and makes a reasonable attempt to answer it. The writer has some idea about how and why Adichie tells her story in the way that she does but the arguments are not taken as far as they might be.

Final word

Notice that the two A* essays on pp. 83–86 use the author's name frequently. In both cases, the candidate has shown that he or she knows that Adichie has created a work of fiction and that it is her work, attitudes and ideas that are being commented on. Some teachers call this 'foregrounding the author' and it is very important if you are aiming for a high grade.

The two grade C essays in this guide do not foreground the author. Instead, the candidates write about Kambili and other characters as if they were real people who think and act for themselves rather than being imagined and presented by an author (although the candidate in Question 2 shows a certain awareness of this in part (b)).

In the examples given above, this is the clearest difference between A* and grade C answers. Foregrounding the author is not difficult. It has been done throughout this guide, especially in the sections on plot, characterisation, themes and style. Look carefully at how the author is focused on and try to do the same thing in your own writing about *Purple Hibiscus.*

Answers

This section provides answers to the 'Review your learning' questions from each of the earlier sections.

Context (p. 18)

1 1960
2 Chinua Achebe.
3 Igbo.
4 Resources such as minerals; ability to grow valuable cash crops such as sugar, cotton etc. and cheap labour to work the land; strategic importance for defence.
5 Imposed initially by the British through schools, churches and government; inevitably universal if all school lessons are in it; useful as a common language across Nigeria. The three main ethnic groups (Igbo, Hausa and Yoruba) each have their own language. English has become the language that cuts across those divisions.
6 They think that no other nation should have invaded, occupied and ruled them — without permission of course — in order to exploit people, natural resources and land.

Plot and structure (p. 31)

1 Jaja defiantly refused to take communion so Papa threw a prayer book at him, which smashed Mama's ornaments.
2 Ifeoma's flat in Nsukka; from Aunty Ifeoma, cousins Amaka, Obiora and Chima, and Father Amadi.
3 The novel is divided into four parts (17 sections).
4 About two years before the Palm Sunday described at the beginning. The novel is structured like an uneven figure of eight, starting with Palm Sunday, then doubling back to describe events leading up to it, then concluding by describing the week or two after Palm Sunday and then nearly three years later.
5 Violent, angry, controlling, proud, wealthy, deeply religious, generous, excessive. All of this is picked up, explained and developed in the 'back story' which forms the main part of the novel.
6 Very British and totally un-African. Represents rejection of African culture by Papa. Without him, Mama will not need them because she

tends to them (a substitute for all those lost babies?) whenever she is nursing injuries caused by his hitting her.

Characterisation (p. 46)

1 She takes away their schedules.
2 They are white. Almost all other characters are black Nigerians.
3 a) Ifediora b) Sisi c) Chima.
4 She has already begun to poison Papa. She says (p. 290) that she began to put the poison in his tea before she went to Nsukka. When Papa picks them up at Nsukka (p. 252), he is already showing the ill effects of it: rash, swollen face etc. Mama has to go back to finish what she has secretly started.
5 Both work closely with/for Kambili's family. Sisi is clearly — although we never see them in conversation — a support and confidante for Mama; she is the only adult in Mama's life who really knows what she suffers. Kevin is essentially Papa's servant, doing jobs for him as well as driving family members to places. He has a mind of his own but is very loyal to Papa. It is as if he and Sisi are on opposite sides of the family and counterbalancing each other.
6 Mama is grateful to be married to Papa. Other girls would have married him readily as he has status and money. Also, she is fond of him despite everything and often comforts him. She seems to see the violence as something she simply has to live with, although she worries about the children (e.g. trying to look after Kambili after the foot scalding). Further, she has nowhere to go. This is all classic psychology of the 'battered wife'. Only after the injuries which put Kambili in hospital does Mama finally take action, but not revenge — she is simply dealing with a problem which she feels simply cannot go on any longer.

Themes (p. 55)

1 She was ten years old.
2 She is feeding her child in his high chair in the same room.
3 He is Nigeria's military dictator after the coup. He is referred to in the *Standard* as 'Big Oga', Igbo term meaning something like 'big boss man'.
4 By mentioning the young girls hawking at the school gate, Adichie highlights the fact that Kambili is a very privileged child who is getting a good, long education in an expensive school. The girls at the gate are younger but do not go to school — they simply try to get a meagre living by selling fruit and other goods to rich people. They are at the

school gate because they know that rich people will come through dropping off their children. Kambili has some sympathy — she notices them and how young they are.

5 Kambili and Jaja are controlled to such an extent that they are not allowed to make decisions at any level for themselves. Even their meals and menus are set out on a schedule. For Amaka, Obiora and Chima, life is tougher — money is short and they have to cope with things such as power and water cuts — but they are growing up to be able to manage their own lives and decide things for themselves.

6 There are various possible answers to this question. Conflict between Christianity and African religions would be a good answer because it is at the root of everything Papa is and does and it affects all the other characters.

Style (p. 67)

1 It is a first-person narrative.
2 Southern Nigeria, east of the river Niger, north of its delta.
3 It is a device to remind the reader that most characters are speaking Igbo most of the time.
4 She often chooses African plants, animals, habits and items as points of comparison, e.g. the flesh on Papa-Nnukwu's arm is compared to a 'brown leather pouch' (p. 167) and Father Benedict's eye colour to that of a snake (p. 105).
5 No specific answer — student's choice.
6 She constantly reminds us which language characters are speaking and how they are using it. Papa's English varies according to his frame of mind. Papa-Nnukwu's dialect is old fashioned. Kambili initially finds Father Amadi's Igbo difficult because it contains more English than she is used to (p. 135).

Tackling the assessments (p. 76)

1 AQA (Assessments and Qualifications Alliance).
2 Foundation-tier questions give you more guidance about what to include in your answer.
3 There is no choice, it is a passage-based question in two parts.
4 Direct quotation; detailed reference to episodes or other features in the novel.
5 Work out what you think the question is asking you to do. Highlight key words in the question. Jot down your main ideas and number them in order or put them on a mini spider diagram.

6 a) Say how you are going to tackle the question, your interpretation of the question or comment on something in it.

b) Summarise your arguments or write a paragraph drawing them together in a different way, including a new point you have held back until the end.

Assessment Objectives and skills (p. 82)

1 They are specific targets to aim for in essays, statements which describe precisely what examiners are looking for.
2 Three.
3 AO1: read critically and imaginatively; AO2: analyse language, structure and form; AO4: relate novel to context.
4 Quality of written communication.
5 A*–C answers are more detailed and analytical. D–G answers tend to be shorter and focus more on what happens in the novel than how it has achieved. (See 'Grade focus' boxes and *Sample essays* section)
6 See list of A* criteria on p. 82.